PRAISE FOR *LEA*

T0357218

"A gifted storyteller delivers provocative, indelible portraits of student after student making leaps in learning that aren't supposed to be possible for children born into trauma."
—Malala Yousafzai, author of *I Am Malala: The Girl Who Stood Up for Education and Was Shot by the Taliban*

"Mufleh . . . chronicles in this magnificent debut how a pickup soccer game transformed her life. . . . Most inspiring, though, is the powerful conviction with which Mufleh writes about supporting those, who, like her, are still fighting for their American dream. . . . Readers will be stunned."
—*Publishers Weekly* (starred review)

"An absorbing account of [Mufleh's] journey from a Jordanian immigrant to an influential educational leader and activist. . . . An impassioned, penetrating critique and inspiring model for progress."
—*Kirkus Reviews* (starred review)

"Luma Mufleh is truly remarkable, inspiring not only to her team of 'Fugees' but to anyone in the world who reads this book. It's a powerful story, reminding us that the journey of refugees and immigrants doesn't end the day they arrive in America. Coach Luma shows us the deep power of one of the world's most universal languages, soccer, and above all the unifying strength of community."
—José Andrés, chef, humanitarian, founder of World Central Kitchen

"This is much more than a book about an inspiring soccer team. It's the story of what schools and sports can do to help heal trauma, foster community, and create opportunities for young people to succeed. To Luma Mufleh's credit, it's also a story about what schools can't do—and shouldn't be expected to do—to overcome society's ills."

—Paul Tough, author of *Whatever It Takes* and
How Children Succeed

"A truly extraordinary story of selflessness, compassion, and the pursuit of justice for one of the most vulnerable communities in our society: refugee children. Luma Mufleh gorgeously weaves her story as a gay Jordanian immigrant living in America and her life-long passion of coaching soccer to better the lives of refugee kids across the country."

—Jose Antonio Vargas, founder of Define American and bestselling
author of *Dear America: Notes of an Undocumented Citizen*

"Luma Mufleh brings her full self to her work, and now, in these pages, to telling the remarkable story of Fugees Family. Our shared American story comes to life in this compelling book."

—Laurene Powell Jobs, founder and president, Emerson Collective

"Luma Mufleh set out to build a soccer team for traumatized young refugees, only to discover the unconscionable neglect they were suffering at the hands of American public education. Then, with inexhaustible humanity, she created a school to make them whole, as learners and as people. Her heartbreaking and ultimately inspiring story illuminates how to remedy educational injustice not only for refugees but also for millions of children born into poverty and trauma in our own country."

—Dale Russakoff, author of the *New York Times* bestseller
The Prize: Who's in Charge of America's Schools?

LEARNING
AMERICA

One Woman's Fight for
Educational Justice
for Refugee Children

LUMA MUFLEH

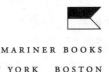

MARINER BOOKS
NEW YORK   BOSTON

For the OG Fugee, my grandmother.

And all Fugees past, present, and future.

LEARNING AMERICA. Copyright © 2022 by Luma Mufleh.
Afterword copyright © 2025 by Luma Mufleh. All rights reserved.
Printed in the United States of America. No part of this book may
be used or reproduced in any manner whatsoever without written
permission except in the case of brief quotations embodied in
critical articles and reviews. For information, address HarperCollins
Publishers, 195 Broadway, New York, NY 10007.

HarperCollins books may be purchased for educational, business,
or sales promotional use. For information, please email the Special
Markets Department at SPsales@harpercollins.com.

The Mariner flag design is a registered trademark of HarperCollins
Publishers LLC.

A hardcover edition of this book was published in 2022 by Mariner
Books.

FIRST MARINER BOOKS PAPERBACK EDITION PUBLISHED 2025.

Designed by Kelly Dubeau Smydra

Library of Congress Cataloging-in-Publication Data
has been applied for.

ISBN 978-0-06-326871-5

25 26 27 28 29 LBC 5 4 3 2 1

CONTENTS

AUTHOR'S NOTE

THE STORIES IN THIS BOOK ARE ALL ABOUT REAL PEOPLE who have helped shape my life. Some of them wanted their names used and others did not. For my students and their families who were concerned about their privacy, I have changed some identifying details.

PROLOGUE

JORDAN IN GEORGIA

I
T WAS A MISTAKE, A WRONG TURN, THAT HAD BROUGHT ME
that spring of 2004 to the parking lot of one of the many shabby
apartment complexes in the refugee resettlement community of
Clarkston, Georgia, twenty miles east of downtown Atlanta. Frustrated and in a hurry, I pulled in to make a U-turn. That's when I saw
them — half a dozen boys, most of them barefoot, passing around a
raggedy soccer ball with two rocks set up for a goal. Everything else
around me ceased to exist.

It was like watching a home movie of my childhood, which I had
spent in neighborhood streets near my home in Amman, Jordan,
kicking a soccer ball between rocks, rarely stopping for water, rest,
or much else. These boys were decent players, but their ball was
half-deflated. A hot breeze pushed garbage beneath broken-down
minivans and across the pavement, which was crumbling, its white
lines faded by the sun.

I've told this story hundreds of times, and it's always a little tough
for Americans to understand. But to me, there was nothing strange
about approaching a group of boys in a parking lot and asking to join
their game. During a pickup match of soccer in the streets of Amman, anyone who wanted to play just had to ask. For the rest of the

world, soccer is a universal language, one that often spans class, racial, and religious divides — as was evident in the lot that day.

At the time, I was coaching a club girls' team for the local YMCA, so I happened to have a bag of new soccer balls in my trunk. I grabbed one and started walking. The boys' game slowed to a halt as they all stopped to stare at me — or, rather, to stare at the ball.

Here's what they didn't say.

Who are you?

What do you want?

Here's what they did say.

"Can we have the ball?"

"I want to play," I answered, indicating that it would be a trade.

The boys exchanged looks and gathered into a huddle. After a few long seconds, they assigned me to a side. It didn't take long to realize they had put me on the weaker team. As the game moved back and forth across the concrete, I called for a pass, and another, but no one would look my way.

I'm not one for showboating, but I realized I would have to prove myself. I stepped up to one of the kids on the opposing team, stripped the ball away from him, and as another player tried to take it away from me, I put it through his legs before easily tapping the ball into the goal.

After that, they took me seriously. We played for hours. It became obvious that most of the kids spoke only a little English, words like "pass" and "shoot" and "goal"; they communicated mostly with hand gestures. We refereed ourselves. I played in my work clothes — cargo pants and a T-shirt — and the boys were wearing a variety of hand-me-downs.

A few days later, at the same time in the afternoon, I drove back to the parking lot. The boys were there, with some new faces and some missing. I grabbed a ball from my car and joined the game. And so it went for weeks; I had found a piece of Jordan in the middle of Georgia.

PART I

WHY DON'T YOU GO BACK?

M Y GRANDMOTHER COMPLETED THE SEVENTH GRADE. That was the end of her formal education. She was married at fifteen and a mother at sixteen. Over the next five years, she gave birth to four more children. None of this was unusual for a middle-class family in Damascus, Syria, in the 1950s.

In 1964, when my grandmother was pregnant with her sixth child, everything changed. Syria was shaken by civil unrest that was followed by a violent military coup. Soldiers occupied nearly every corner of Damascus's ancient streets. Syrians were pitted against one another: urban against rural, merchants against farmers, brother against brother. This is what a civil war does; it unstitches the fabric of a country and tears apart the colors and textures that made it beautiful in the first place.

She didn't need a diploma to know that something was very wrong now, that she could no longer keep her children safe. Call it a survival instinct or a mother's special way of knowing; whatever it was, it made her — pregnant belly and all — pack five children into the family car and drive away from the only home she had ever known. Only 129 miles separate Damascus and Amman, but they were the difference between life and death.

My grandfather stayed behind, believing that things would blow over, like the time before and the time before that. There had always been unrest, talk of change. There was no reason for alarm, he insisted; surely his wife and children would be back soon.

Instead, two months later, my grandfather followed the same dusty highway to Amman. His factories had been seized by the government. His brothers had been tortured. Syria was unrecognizable, a police state.

My mother — my grandmother's firstborn — was sixteen years old when the family fled to Jordan. Her whole world had been taken away: the country she loved, the extended family and the apartment building they all shared, her school, and her friends. For a while, she told herself that the move was just temporary, that they would stay in Jordan for a few months then return to Damascus; surely things would go back to normal in Syria soon. But at her parents' insistence, she enrolled in school in Amman.

It didn't go well. Classmates and teachers alike mocked her French-inflected Syrian accent, her halting English (Jordan, having been colonized by the British, was an English- and Arabic-speaking society while neighboring Syria primarily spoke French and Arabic). To this day, my mother understands English perfectly well but refuses to speak it in almost any setting.

Even though Jordan and Syria share a border and many cultural similarities, my mother was immediately identified and treated as other, as different, as less than. At first, she fought back. She told her classmates that Syria was the better country anyway.

"Then why don't you go back?" they retorted.

After a few months, she refused to go to school. My grandparents didn't know what to do. They weren't going to let her drop out. They were committed to making sure every one of their children had an education, something fairly rare in the region at that time.

"Please go to school today, it will get better, just give it time," they begged.

"It won't. I hate it here. Why can't we go home? Please, let's go home."

My grandparents were torn. My mother was unhappy, but she was safe. She was in school, but she was not learning. They had made it out of Syria, unlike so many of their neighbors, but would they ever truly belong in this new place?

They eventually gave in and sent my mother back to Syria to finish high school. She would live with her aunt for two years until she graduated and returned to Jordan—that was the plan. For a brief moment, things were as good as they could be for her. She was without her siblings and her parents, but she was home. She returned to her beloved Catholic school, overjoyed to see the teachers and friends she had left behind.

My mother's reclaimed normalcy was short-lived. The regime soon began shutting down all nongovernment schools. She remembers standing on the playground as she watched armed soldiers march the nuns out of the building—as if they were criminals, these women who had taught her how to read and write. She remembers the moment when she and her classmates ran to them, begging them not to go. The soldiers tried to place their rifles between the girls and the nuns, but the teenagers would not be deterred. They were determined to say goodbye at least. Syria would never be the same.

I was born in 1975 in Amman, a place constantly in the cross fire of regional violence. I don't remember a time during my childhood when there wasn't a conflict swelling or a war unfolding in a bordering country. Because of my family's wealth and Jordan's good relationship with the United States, we enjoyed some semblance of normalcy. But the drums of war always beat steadily in the background, and we knew implicitly that our lives could be upended overnight.

My parents put me in an Arabic-speaking school when I was five. I think they did it to resist the lingering colonialist influence in the region, the idea that the West did things better than everyone else.

They were fiercely Arab; sending me to an Arab school, in many ways, was an act of patriotism. But as with most parents, their commitment to an ideal went only as far as their own child's well-being. After a teacher struck me with a ruler for speaking out of turn, my mother immediately pulled me out of the school.

I began attending a school run by the British embassy. My first few weeks were difficult, to say the least. In my family, we spoke only Arabic. All of a sudden, I was sitting in a class where instruction and conversation happened completely in English. The only kids I had ever interacted with were Arab kids; now my classmates were from all over the world: Japan, India, England, Nigeria, Scotland, Switzerland. Unlike my old teachers, these teachers didn't wear a hijab, and their skirts ended at the knee. My PE teacher wore shorts.

I would come home complaining of pounding headaches, telling my parents that I just wanted to go to sleep. My mom was worried that she was watching her daughter relive her own terrible experience. She would ask my dad if they should consider switching me again. "Just give it time; she's young," he would reassure her.

For a while, I faked my way through. I excelled in — and loved — the classes that didn't require me to speak English. In art, I could draw by copying what the teacher was showing us. In PE, I could run and throw a ball without having to say a word. And in music, I could sing at the top of my lungs because I was simply imitating a sound; what the song meant, I had no idea. Eventually, through total immersion and the dedication of truly wonderful teachers, I began to learn English. I began to love school.

I attended a British dual-language middle school and went on to an American high school. When I was applying to college, British and American universities were the only ones I considered. I believed very strongly that Western education was the best the world had to offer and that everyone who lived in those countries had received an education like mine. I thought that the disrespect and parochialism my mother had experienced in her Amman school didn't happen in developed countries.

In addition to her aversion to English, my mother still bristles when I call her a refugee. To her, that word is heavy with shame and suffering, and she is quick to downplay her own ordeal. It's true, despite all of the loss and the trauma, that our family was profoundly lucky. But our history shaped us and continues to shape us today.

When I was eight years old, my grandmother took me to a Palestinian refugee camp outside Amman. It was important to her that I understand our family's journey, how easily things could have been different for us. At first, I was terrified. I had never seen anything like this place — rows and rows of tents shaking in the unrelenting desert wind, everything in sight a shade of brown.

My grandmother had brought things for the women at the camp, clothes and food, and she told me to go play while she visited with them. Still hiding behind her legs, I refused.

"I don't want to play," I said. "I want to stay with you."

My grandmother knelt down beside me, and with a sternness she seldom used, said: "Don't ever think people are beneath you, and don't think you have nothing to learn from others. Go."

I did as I was told. I walked hesitantly to the sidelines of a pickup game of soccer on the camp's makeshift field. After a few moments, one of the kids waved me in. Soon, my fear was gone, replaced by a feeling of camaraderie. These kids were no different from me despite how they looked or where they lived.

After a few hours of playing, I ran to find my grandmother. I couldn't wait to tell her how much fun I'd had; I wanted her to be proud of me.

"*Haram*," I said, as we walked out of the camp. *Poor them.*

"*Haram* on us," my grandmother said, using the word in a different way — that we were sinning. "Don't feel sorry for them. Believe in them."

Today, a staggering seventy million people have been forced to leave their homes due to war, persecution, or human rights violations — the highest levels in recorded history. Only .01 percent of them will ever be resettled. These are numbers that are hard to get your head around and a problem that's too easy to dismiss as someone else's.

Historically, the United States has admitted more refugees than any other country, but the number of people we resettle has been tumbling for years. From 2016 to 2020, refugee resettlement in America dropped nearly 85 percent, from approximately 85,000 people to slightly more than 11,000 at the end of the Trump administration. As I write this, the Biden administration appears to be reversing course after critics slammed its initial 2021 refugee cap of 15,000, the lowest in history.

You don't have to be particularly news savvy to read or hear the word "refugee" often. Yet the refugee resettlement system in the United States remains a mystery for many of us. Perhaps your community has a large Somali or Iraqi population. Perhaps you've always wondered how they came to live in your city.

Here's how it typically unfolds in this country. After a years-long and invasive screening process, the United Nations High Commissioner for Refugees recommends an applicant for resettlement in the United States based on their circumstances and the danger they face in their home country. Each refugee or refugee family is then assigned to one of the nine domestic resettlement agencies that have a cooperative agreement with the US Department of State. Some of those agencies are familiar to us, large organizations like the International Rescue Committee or Catholic Charities; others are smaller affiliates. Their job is to facilitate refugees' journeys to America and their first months in the country, picking them up at the airport, securing an apartment, and helping them find a job — checking all the logistical boxes. Resettlement agencies aren't created equal, though, and a positive experience often hinges on the tireless, thankless work of resettlement workers.

Today, the majority of refugees come from African countries, but that is largely due to the Trump administration's travel ban, a policy that sharply limited the number of refugees accepted from Syria, Yemen, and other places in the Middle East. Refugees are resettled in just about every state in the nation, in smaller cities like Columbus, Des Moines, Omaha, Fort Wayne, Louisville, and Nashville, and in larger ones like New York, Houston, Atlanta, and Chicago. Visit any of these "resettlement hubs," and you're likely to find enclaves of Burmese, Afghan, or Eritrean refugees quietly forging new lives after surviving some of the world's most brutal conflicts. By virtue of their refugee status, they are lucky. Lottery-winner lucky. But resettlement is not a red carpet. It is not a free ride. Many of the cities where refugees wind up aren't prepared to welcome them, their institutions and infrastructure woefully ill-equipped to facilitate successful resettlement. Many refugees spend their first years in America contending with crippling loneliness, crumbling apartment buildings, and school systems that have no idea what to do with them or their children. Belonging, healing, hope — there are no checkboxes for those things.

More than a third of refugees are children. Their introduction to the United States comes in newcomer centers, academic programs funded and administered by local school districts where, in theory, kids receive help learning to read and write English before being placed in general education classrooms. Like resettlement agencies, newcomer centers are often overwhelmed, understaffed, and suffer from ill-defined standards and vague mission statements. This is evident in the performance of refugee students once they're mainlined into traditional schools, where they face language barriers and bullying, and are five times more likely to drop out than their native-born peers.

But I didn't know any of this that day in the parking lot. I didn't realize that these stories were playing out all around me in my American city, that refugee hands had cleaned my hotel rooms and packaged my chicken, that the players I coached sat next to refugee students in their urban classrooms. Even though I was a foreign-born daughter of refugees, those seventy million people were just numbers to me, too. Until I learned their names.

2

THE FUGEES

HABIBULLAH, NABIULLAH, AND AZIZULLAH (HABIB, NABI, and Aziz) were Afghan brothers. Tall and sinewy, Majok was from South Sudan. He was one of the fastest kids I had ever seen. Sulayman, a sturdy boy with a massive smile, came from The Gambia. Jerome was from Liberia—the boys called him One Shoe because he played with one black oversize sneaker on his kicking foot. Jerome was serious about taking care of that sneaker; he wiped it down after every practice and always changed into his flip-flops for the two-mile walk home.

The boys, some of whom had Muslim names, heard something familiar in my voice as I repeated their names back to them. It had been a while since anyone outside their family had pronounced them properly.

I told them I was a soccer coach.

"You coach professional?" one boy asked.

"No, kids about your age," I explained.

"What do we need to do to have a team?" they asked.

"Well, we'll need a field."

"We know where all the fields are! We'll show you!"

"We'll need referees."

At this, they jeered. "We don't need referees!"

"And we'll need more kids."

We piled in my car and drove slowly up and down the streets of Clarkston looking for kids of a certain height. When we spotted one, I'd slow my bright yellow Beetle to a crawl and the boys would call out to them. If our potential recruit spoke a language that none of us knew, we'd hold up a soccer ball and five fingers to indicate the time we'd be playing. I'm not sure if it's crazier that the kids we approached weren't all that fazed or that this plan actually worked. We soon had recruited enough players to put together a real team.

But this wasn't a Disney movie. We weren't the Mighty Ducks or even the Bad News Bears. My reality got complicated very quickly.

At the time, the bulk of my reality took place at the café I had just opened. I had been living in America for nearly ten years. During my senior year of college in 1997, I had applied for asylum as part of a protected social group — as a gay woman, it would have been dangerous, possibly fatal, for me to return to Jordan. When my father learned that I was gay — and that I wasn't coming home — he and the rest of my family (except for my grandmother) cut me off financially and emotionally. The café was going to be my redemption story; I was going to live the American dream *and* prove to my parents that I could make it on my own.

I shopped around for spaces, eventually settling on an old garage in Decatur's business district. Oil stains marred the floor and every hour or so a train rumbled by on the tracks out front. I thought that the building had potential, with its exposed beams and excess of natural light, and the idea that I would create something from nothing was delightful. I drew up a business plan and recruited investors: parents of the girls I coached or former classmates from Smith College, where I had gone to school. I chose the paint colors and stayed up until the early hours applying coat after coat myself. I hung paintings by local artists and light fixtures that looked like fat, fluffy clouds. I called the café Ashton's after a friend's dog, a name I knew would earn us top billing in the yellow pages.

Starting the team felt a lot like starting the café — exhausting but exciting. I had been coaching for many years — during high school in Jordan and again when I moved to Atlanta after college, but somewhere along the line I had lost my passion for it. After state championships and all-star rosters, I wasn't sure what was left for me to accomplish. Establishing a team from the ground up felt like a challenge I could sink my teeth into.

The first thing I did was have the boys sign a code of conduct, just as I had with all the teams I coached. I had found that laying out the rules early and requiring the kids to sign a "contract" helped establish cohesion and made them more accountable. It also made them feel important, like they were a part of something bigger than themselves.

Players were expected to show up on time if they wanted to play — the minute my cleats stepped on the field, the boys had to be warmed up and ready to go. If they were going to be late, *they* had to call ahead, not their mom or their dad (though I would learn that many of these boys' parents didn't speak English, nor did they live to drive their sons to and from their extracurriculars like those of many of my former players). To simplify things and ensure camaraderie, the boys had to speak English at practice. If you spoke in a language that only a few understood, you made others feel excluded and ostracized, which is not conducive to building a strong team.

Appearance mattered. No saggy pants and the boys' hair was to be short and brushed. Uniforms were to be spotless. Everywhere the boys went, they were to remember that they represented the entire team now.

Those were the standards I had held all my players to. For this team, I thought that this was doubly important. As an immigrant, I knew the way people looked at me when they learned I was Arab. I was used to the double takes and long stares people gave me when they found out I was also Muslim. Most Americans have felt that kind of pressure only on a first date. For minorities, every day is a first date.

As a light-skinned woman with no discernible accent, I could pass. Most of my players couldn't. I wanted them to understand that people were going to judge them based on how they presented themselves. If they showed up to the field with dirty clothes, unbrushed hair, and saggy pants, that sent a message: *I don't care about myself.* And it gave others permission not to care about them either. They were going to have to work twice as hard to earn people's respect — on and off the field — so they had to respect themselves first.

Last but not least, I would be checking everyone's report cards. If you were failing any class, you were on the bench until you got your grades up. No excuses, no exceptions.

"Alright guys, we need a name," I told them one day after practice. They were passing around my water bottle, which had quickly become a community water bottle.

"How about the All-Stars?" one of them said.

I laughed and raised an eyebrow. "You guys think you're all-stars?"

"Yeah, not really," someone mumbled. We had been practicing together for weeks; they knew there would be no ego trips on this team.

"How about Manchester United?" Now they were trying to get a rise out of me.

"Not Manchester United — Chelsea!" said another. At this, I got some brownnosing grins.

"We can't name ourselves after another team!" I said. "We have to be our own team."

The boys fell quiet.

"What about the Fugees?" I posed. I had seen the band in college when most of the boys were small children living through a war or confined in a refugee camp.

"The Fugees?" A dozen furrowed brows looked my way. "What's that?"

"Well, we are all refugees, so — Fugees."

"Wait, we are *all* refugees?" They looked at one another. Until that moment, our identities as outsiders had gone unspoken.

"Cool! We are the Fugees!" And that was that.

To register for the YMCA league we would be playing in, the boys needed to submit forms with their personal information. I didn't have time to send the forms home to parents, so I sat the boys in a circle and one by one completed the paperwork, calling out each question and writing down the answers as they came. "Full name?" I said, and the boys took turns spelling their names. "Address?" I said, and they recited their apartment numbers. Then I asked for birthdays.

"One, one, nineteen ninety-two," said one.

"One, one, nineteen ninety-three," said the next.

"Are you guys just copying each other?" I looked up from the stack of papers rustling in the hot wind.

"No! That's my birthday," the boys said together.

"Wait — do you want my real birthday or my fake birthday?" said Sidi.

The confusion must have been visible on my face because he explained, "I told them my birthday, but my mom didn't have the right papers. So they said my birthday was January first."

I knew enough to assume that "they" meant asylum or UN officers. It seemed that nearly everyone on the team was "born" on New Year's Day or Christmas Day except for a small handful born on the Fourth of July.

Because none of them had extended family or friends in the country, I wrote my own name for each boy's emergency contact.

The Fugees needed uniforms, so on a sunny Saturday afternoon Habib, Nabi, Aziz, and Jerome crowded into my Beetle, and we drove down Memorial Drive, the ugly six-lane road that bisects Atlanta. The Sock Man, as he was known, sold discount socks and T-shirts on the weekends out of his white van; a canopy tent and folding table comprised a makeshift storefront. The boys stood quietly as I haggled with the guy, ultimately snagging twenty white T-shirts and twenty pairs of black socks for fourteen dollars.

At the next practice, everyone got a T-shirt and their turn with a black permanent marker. I assigned numbers based on positions, and the boys clumsily drew them on the back of their shirts. They asked if they could design a Fugees logo for the front, but I decided against it; I expected the lopsided numbers would earn us enough derision from opposing teams.

To complete the uniform, I asked my former players—all teenage girls—to donate their black shorts from last year's season as well as any cleats or shin guards they could part with. The Fugees were pumped to receive new-to-them cleats. They happily wore shoes that were two sizes too big. We didn't gather enough shin guards for everyone, so the remaining players simply tucked cardboard into their socks. Like my water bottle, shin guards became community property, the boys switching them at halftime. The majority of them had never played in shin guards anyway.

Finally, it was September. Our first game was on a Saturday morning, so that Friday at practice I took a few minutes to run through the formalities of a YMCA match. I told the boys about equipment checks and how they should line up after the game to high-five the opposing team no matter the outcome. The Fugees listened politely, but I could tell their minds were elsewhere: this would be their first game with uniforms, a referee, and people cheering (albeit no one for us). This was big time, the closest to playing in the World Cup they would ever come.

"I couldn't sleep last night!" a few players told me when we met at our practice field on Saturday. Others were quiet but I could tell by their posture that they were nervous, anxious, and amped up. Looking at them, I also became anxious. I began to worry that I had underestimated our ability to meet the gravity of this moment.

There wasn't a lot of time to worry, though. Because we didn't have a bus or carpooling parents, I would be shuttling everyone to the field in my car. After the first five piled into the Beetle, I sent the rest of the team jogging toward our destination to save time; I would drive back and pick them up in shifts.

We got some looks at the field. As a female coach with fifteen minority players in a league where male coaches were the rule and white kids the majority, I had expected that. What had become normal for us was unusual and even bizarre outside our bubble. The other team snickered as the referee struggled to announce our roster. I had hoped that these slights would encourage the Fugees to play harder, but the opposite happened; they fell apart.

They yelled at one another. They abandoned their positions. They hogged the ball, each of them trying to be the star, none of them trusting their teammates. They theatrically fell down and pretended to be "injured" like they had seen their favorite players do on TV. They called the ref a cheater. They allowed goal after goal and loudly blamed the goalie and one another. We got pounded.

The loss was an eye-opener for me. These kids had tremendous raw talent but lacked the confidence, trust, and discipline I had taken for granted in my former players. Many of them loved soccer more than anything in the world — had come up watching, playing, and dreaming about it — but had no idea about the off-field habits that make good players great.

"What did you do wrong?" I asked at the end of the game. The finger-pointing began.

"He missed thirty shots!"

"I would have made that goal!"

"He let everyone run past him!"

"I didn't ask what *he* did, I asked what *you* did," I barked. "Take responsibility for what *you* did."

I practiced what I preached. I adapted practice so instead of spending fifteen minutes going over the formalities of a match, we often spent twice that long, covering them again and again. I wanted my players to feel perfectly comfortable lining up for equipment checks (even if they were hiding cardboard in their socks) or hearing their names on the field. I also hammered home the importance of pregame rituals: packing your bag before bed, eating a carb-heavy dinner and a protein-rich breakfast. If those foods weren't available (and for some of my players, they weren't) they were to drink a lot of water and avoid sugar. No gas station snacks before games. Get plenty of sleep.

To show them what humility and teamwork looked like up close, I asked my former girls' team to scrimmage with the Fugees the Friday before their second game.

"I thought this would be an easy way to end the week," I lied. The boys took their positions looking smug and self-assured. A scrimmage against a bunch of girls? They thought that this would be a breeze.

The girls walloped them. More important, the girls walloped them while working together as a team. There was no yelling or finger-pointing. When one of the girls made a mistake, her team shook it off, no big deal. When one person scored, everyone celebrated. When a player was knocked down, her teammates were the first to pick her up.

"What did you notice about the way they played?" I asked the Fugees after the game. A dozen dejected faces looked back. "You played against a team, not one superstar," I said. "No one was fighting for time or hogging the ball."

I then asked each one of them to pick up a stick or a twig from a tree and bring it to me. Each stick, I told them, represented the player. When they returned, I took one of the sticks and easily snapped it in half. I took another two and snapped those in half just as effortlessly. Then I arranged eleven sticks between my hands.

"Eleven sticks — eleven players on a team," I said. The boys watched intently. I tried to break the sticks in half as I had with the others but I couldn't. I handed the sticks to Sulayman and asked him to break them. He couldn't.

"Each one of you alone is breakable. Even two or three of you together. But all eleven? Strong and united — no one can break that. Not on the field. Not off."

The Fugees lost their second game but not as badly as the first one. They squeaked out a win in their third. By the middle of the season, they were routinely blowing other teams out of the water. They also got better at dealing with the disparagement they received. We attracted attention everywhere we went. After games, opposing coaches asked my players, "Where is your coach?" and the boys would point to me. "No, your *real* coach," they would say.

More often though, it was the other players who hurled insults and slurs at the Fugees. During one game, it got so bad that I approached the referee about it. He pretended not to have heard.

At halftime, I told the kids not to let the other team get in their heads. The best revenge was winning the game and winning it big.

"If they call you bad names or you start feeling angry," I said, "just walk away and smile."

One of my Sierra Leonean players, Joseph, spoke so little English that the only word he gleaned from my pep talk was "smile." So smile he did. When the opposing coach started yelling from the sidelines, Joseph stopped, turned to him, and smiled. This made the coach yell more, which made Joseph smile even bigger. Finally, the coach exploded.

"What are you looking at, boy? Turn your nigger-ass face away from me!"

The ref heard that one. The coach was ejected, and Joseph just smiled. We won the game 7–3.

———

I showed up to practice one day to find the field deserted. I was confused, since these kids never missed a chance to play soccer. I stepped out of my car when two boys emerged from behind a dumpster, waving their hands frantically and running toward me.

"Habib got jumped! There was blood everywhere," they said. "These bad kids beat him up."

"Where is he?" I asked, half expecting him to be behind the dumpster.

"He went to his house. Everyone else left—they were all scared!"

I hopped into my car and drove to the apartment complex. Nabi answered the door and told me that Habib was refusing to come out of the boys' room.

The apartment was cramped but tidy. Black and red rugs and cushions covered the floor, and a poster that said ALLAH in Arabic calligraphy hung on the wall.

"Habib? Come on out; I need to check on you," I said. "To see if you are okay." Habib's face appeared in his doorway; his lips were split and swollen; a gash cut through his hairline.

I was calm as I inspected Habib's cuts. They were probably nothing that an ice pack and ibuprofen couldn't fix, but I knew that he needed to be taken to the hospital—just in case.

"Where's your mom? Is she home?" I asked.

"Mother *joon*!" the boys called.

When Shaida emerged from her own room, I was still facing Habib, my back turned to her. Suddenly, the walls echoed with her terrified Farsi. Alarmed, I spun around just as the boys—all three of them—fell to the ground laughing. I was speechless. The boys' mother rushed back into her bedroom and reappeared, now wrestling with her headscarf.

"She's saying, 'I thought you said your coach was a Muslim woman!'" Nabi told me through a giant smile. From behind, I didn't appear to be either to her, and Muslim women who wear a head-scarf are prohibited from showing their hair in the presence of a man.

"I am Muslim," I said. To convince her, I offered the Muslim declaration of faith: *Ashadu an la ilaha illallah wa ashadu anna Muhammadan Rasulullah.* Shaida's eyes registered relief, and maybe some lingering confusion, as she realized that the unveiled, shorts-wearing, American-looking woman was telling the truth.

"Will you tell your mom that you should probably go to the hospital," I said to Habib.

He translated. Her response included the words "insurance" and "no." Shaida, not five feet tall, was draped in an Afghan housedress. Her dark hair spilled out from underneath the half-wrapped scarf.

"Our insurance isn't working . . ." Habib said.

"We can deal with that. They still have to take care of you and most kids in Georgia get free health insurance if they need it."

He spoke quickly to his mother in Farsi, then Shaida fell silent, deliberating.

"It's probably nothing to worry about." I pointed to my head, not sure if she would understand. "But with head injuries, we should play it safe."

"Okay. You go."

"Me?"

"Yes. You go and Habib."

"Oh, no. You should take him."

"Me no go hospital. You go."

So we went. When we got to the hospital, Habib and I sat together to fill out his intake form. He wrote down his name and I completed the rest.

"Now we wait a long time," he said, after he returned the clipboard to the receptionist.

I walked up to the desk and explained to the young woman working there that my player had a head injury and that we needed to be seen right away. The woman sorted through the clipboards to find

Habib's paperwork, and five minutes later, we were in an examination room. Habib needed a few stitches, a few ibuprofens, and some rest. Other than that, he was okay.

"It's never been that quick," Habib said on the drive home. "The nurses and doctors don't usually listen to people like that."

"We probably got lucky and got a nice person," I said. I didn't think too much at the time about what had actually happened that night. About why my player had gotten attacked on the way to practice. Or about how Habib's family typically spent hours at the hospital waiting or how they might not go at all because they were afraid of problems with their insurance.

Back at the apartment complex, I had intended to drop Habib off and finally get back to work at the café. But before I could drive away, Shaida came out onto the sidewalk and waved for me to come inside. She had prepared a feast: *mantu, daal,* rice, and freshly baked bread.

3

THE LUCKY ONES

INNERS WITH SHAIDA AND HER CHILDREN BECAME A regular event. We ate on the floor around Shaida's delicious food spread out on a plastic tablecloth. The cheap light dangling from the popcorn ceiling made harsh shadows on the walls, but the room felt full and warm. On these nights, we mostly talked about school, work, or other Afghan families in Clarkston, the boys serving as interpreters, but one night, out of nowhere, Shaida said, "Taliban, no good."

I had never asked Shaida questions about Afghanistan or the family's journey to America. I knew firsthand the kind of feelings those questions evoked. It doesn't matter what forces you to leave your country — war, religious persecution, or economic necessity — the experience of surviving is marked by a thousand small deaths. A home you'll never see again, severed family ties, and a gnawing sense of guilt over those left behind.

"Yes, Taliban isn't good." I nodded my head to agree with her.

"Very bad," she said.

"Why very bad?"

Shaida abandoned her attempts at English and began to speak in Farsi. When she paused, her oldest children, Sheema, Habib, and

Nabi, would converse in Farsi until they agreed on the English translation. Eight-year-old Aziz hardly remembered the journey and sat listening as earnestly as I did.

"You know we live in Afghanistan, then go to Pakistan. Taliban very bad," Shaida began. "You know I have older son, Jahan."

"Yes, the boys mentioned that." I took a deep breath, hoping Jahan was alive.

"We sent him to another country so he won't die."

My relief for Jahan was short-lived.

"After, they took uncle and dad." Shaida's brother and husband. Disappeared like thousands of men and women all over Afghanistan during the Taliban's rise to power in the nineties. Their family was targeted because not only were they Shiite, the religious minority, they were also Hazara, an ethnic minority with Mongolian ancestry that made the family appear more Asian than Semitic.

The irony was not lost on me that Shaida was sharing her family's story — while literally breaking bread — with a Sunni Muslim. It was devastating to think that these atrocities were committed in the name of our faith.

Many family members fled to Pakistan, but Shaida stayed. Because the Taliban targets teenage boys, Shaida felt that, with Jahan gone, her younger boys and daughter were safe. *What,* I wondered, *had happened to the dad and uncle?*

"Father dead. Taliban kill father and uncle," the boys interpreted. Shaida spoke matter-of-factly, showing little emotion.

"Coach, they kills them in soccer field," Nabi said.

I had read about the killings in soccer fields. The Taliban would line up men and women parallel to the penalty spot and execute them in front of a stadium filled with people, some of whom came willingly, others who were forced to watch. These killings sent a powerful message: the Taliban could do whatever they wanted wherever they wanted.

While they settled on translations, I studied the family, the boys'

shiny black hair, Shaida's silky headscarf. This was not a news article, something I could shudder at and click away from. These were
real people. Real kids who had lost their father, a real woman who
had lost a husband and a brother. Worse, they knew exactly how.
Lined up on a soccer pitch in front of thousands of people and shot
for nothing, their blood draining into the dirt.

Every person has a different breaking point, the moment when
they know in their bones that it's time to go. For some, it's the first
rumblings of war; for others, it's a direct threat to their life or the
lives of those they love. Others stay until every building around them
is nothing but rubble. Nobody wants to leave their home.

Shaida's breaking point happened in a grocery store a few weeks
after her husband was killed. She and Nabi, who was five at the time,
had gone to get food. Any time Shaida left the house, she was careful
to cover herself in a burka, as mandated for all women by the Taliban. At the market, though, she reached out for a tomato and inadvertently exposed a sliver of her wrist. A man nearby began yelling.
He had a long beard and wore a military uniform. He revealed a cut-
up water hose, the Taliban's weapon of choice to punish those who
violated religious law.

Nabi watched helplessly as the man viciously whipped his mother's ankles and wrists. He held her weight with his small body as
they hobbled home. Now Shaida was ready to leave.

The bus that took them from their home in Kabul boarded at 3
a.m. Early mornings were the safest times to leave, though no time
was truly safe. It was standing room only; there was barely enough
space for the one small suitcase the family was sharing. The sight
of a mother with small children had earned them a spot on the bus.
They paid their money to a driver wearing an olive turban and a long
beard.

"Me no like beard," Shaida paused to say.

"I don't like the beard either," I said.

"Beard no good."

"Beards are bad," I agreed.

We were both referring to the long beards common among conservative Muslims and universal for the Taliban, which had banned shaving. In fact, several Muslim sects believe that it is wrong to shave despite the Quran's silence on the matter.

As the bus rumbled out of town, Shaida's family was squeezed and jostled around on the bumpy roads that had been bombed throughout the war. The kids held on to their mother, who at four foot nine inches was then the tallest member of her family. The inside was so crammed with people that several men rode atop the bus. A few hours in, Shaida remembered, the bus started smelling like onions as people sweated out their dinner. At the rest stops, people rinsed their clothes, washed their faces, and drank from dirty streams.

After twelve hours, the bus was stopped close to the border with Pakistan. Taliban soldiers surrounded the bus and yelled for everyone to get off. They fired warning shots into the air.

All the belongings and bags were tossed off the bus and the soldiers rifled through them, taking whatever caught their fancy. The rest of it they left splayed out in the dirt. Some of the younger men were led away.

When they had taken what they wanted, the soldiers demanded payment. Twenty dollars a person. Those who could pay reboarded the bus. Those who couldn't were detained. Shaida didn't have enough money for every child. She deliberated about sending two of them on the bus but couldn't decide on which two. Ultimately, she concluded that it was best for them to stick together.

They were taken to a small containment area, a slab of concrete surrounded by barbed wire. It smelled strongly of urine, and there were no toilets or running water. Shaida remembered babies crying, people throwing up in the squalor. The family found a corner and huddled there, as far from the puddles of urine and feces as they could manage.

"We eat." Shaida brought her hand to her face.

I must have looked confused because she sent Nabi into the kitchen. He came back holding a date.

"You ate dates," I said.

"Date?" Shaida repeated.

"Yes, date."

"Three week we eat date," Shaida said.

People began arriving at the area, circling the fence to try to find family members and pay for their release. Shaida was relieved when her cousin's face appeared in that crowd. He paid fifty dollars to get them out and drove them to Islamabad in his rickshaw. There was a tiny unfurnished bedroom waiting for them in Pakistan.

"Coach, you know the thing we saws in the store?" Nabi interrupted.

Earlier that week, I had taken some of the boys on an errand on the way to practice. At a furniture store, they had seen a carpet loom displayed on the wall. They excitedly pointed at it, explaining that they knew how to use one. I had assumed they meant that their mom knew how to use one.

"Yes," I said. "The carpet loom."

The boys explained that they made carpets during their time in Pakistan to earn money. They could produce a hand-sewn rug in one month, which Shaida would take to the market and sell to a wholesaler for one hundred dollars, enough to allow the family to live until the next month. For two years they did this. The kids were better at making the rugs than the adults because they were faster. Their young hands and brains could adapt a lot quicker to the motions that were needed.

"It's like learning English," Nabi explained. "The younger you are, the easier."

During those two years, the family applied for resettlement in the United States. Several of their family members did, too. The process included five interviews during which they were taken into separate rooms and asked identical questions. The interviewers were looking for any inconsistencies in their stories. Aziz, the youngest, was six at the time. On five separate occasions, he was isolated and asked to recount the brutality and terror he had witnessed in Afghanistan and on his family's journey to Pakistan. He was asked about his murdered father. He was asked how he could be sure that his father was really dead.

They were the lucky ones. They got approved. No other family member did.

They landed in New York City at 11 p.m. on a steamy July night in 2002. A resettlement worker met them at the airport. He did not speak Farsi, and no one in the family could speak English yet. He dropped them off at a hotel with a wave and a bucket of chicken. The next morning, he arrived at their door and told them that it was time to leave.

"But we just got here," they tried to tell him. The family had mistakenly thought the hotel was their new home. They were confused but hurriedly repacked their suitcase and followed the resettlement worker downstairs, where they ate their first American breakfast — cereal and donuts. Then it was back to the airport. They had no idea where they were going.

In Atlanta, they were greeted by yet another caseworker who didn't speak Farsi. Finally, they were delivered to a sparsely furnished apartment in Clarkston. They were left for a week with a bag of groceries and no further instructions, no support, no help. The world outside their window looked alien and calm and very green. They didn't have to worry about their safety; the Taliban would never be able to walk into their apartment here. They were free.

Still, the adjustment was far from easy. The kids were mocked in school because they looked different, spoke no English, and wore their Afghan clothes. Sometimes they got beat up. They had never attended school in Afghanistan or Pakistan, so academically they lagged far behind. Meanwhile, Shaida spent most days cleaning rooms at the Marriott in Stone Mountain.

Shaida and her children told me this story that night without a single complaint. Not about the way they were treated at school, not about the work conditions Shaida endured, not about the safety of their apartment. When Shaida fell through the floor and landed in the laundry room, sustaining injuries that prevented her from working, they simply moved, ate rice and beans for a month, and built themselves back up. As bad as things got sometimes, nothing was as bad as what they had left behind.

"We lucky," Shaida said with a smile.

"We are very lucky," I agreed.

On the way home that night, I thought about Shaida and the children on that crowded bus. I thought about how relieved she must have felt to be escaping but also how terrified, how sad. It was a feeling I knew; one I had tried very hard to forget. Whenever anyone asked me how I ended up in the United States, my reply was queued up and ready to go: "I went to college here and stayed."

There isn't one moment I can point to when I became sure about my choice to apply for asylum, just as there isn't one moment I can point to when I knew that I was gay. In fact, there isn't even a word for "gay" in Arabic. I may not have had a name for the feelings I had as a teenager in the Middle East, but I knew enough to keep them a secret.

As progressive as Jordan may seem to the outside world, it is still primarily a Muslim country, unchanged by reformation. An average of twenty women a year are killed in Jordan because they have dishonored their families (those are just the reported cases — the number is likely much higher) through adultery, sex outside of marriage, or being gay. Often it is only the rumor of this behavior that dooms these women. They are burned, beaten, shot, or stabbed to death, and there are often few or no consequences for the family members involved. I grew up in this culture of fear, reading about, hearing about, and witnessing violence against women in the name of family honor. At the age of seventeen, I was held at gunpoint and terrorized by a police officer who had found me kissing a woman in the park. Surviving that encounter was a fluke. If I stayed in Jordan, I had no doubt that the next time I wouldn't be as lucky.

The news that I had been granted asylum came in August of 1997 after an excruciating (and expensive) process that took up the entirety of my senior year at Smith. It was a harrowing time, to say the least, full of lawyers and stomachaches and even more secrets from my family. After a decade of hiding my sexuality, I was now required to *prove* it, soliciting old girlfriends to write sworn statements about our intimate relationships for immigration authorities to peruse. Friends also provided testimonials and I wrote my own, stating at the end: *Sometimes I wish I had a choice. A choice of being straight. Because if I had the choice, I would choose not to dishonor my family. I would choose not to be raped by a husband. I would choose not to be killed by my family and my government. I would choose to live in Jordan.*

When I learned that the United States would take me in, I was overwhelmed by two conflicting emotions: profound relief and deep sorrow. I had ensured my physical safety — but it would cost me everything: my country, my family, my life as I knew it.

A few weeks after my asylum decision, I sat on the floor of a friend's apartment in Detroit, where I had gone when my summer job at Smith came to an end. With her cat perched in my lap, I dialed the parade of numbers on the back of a calling card.

I spoke to my father in Arabic until I ran out of words. Then, finally, I said it: "I'm gay." I said it again. I said it over and over. My mother got on the phone. They pleaded with me to come home.

They said I had been brainwashed. They said I had joined a cult. After we hung up, they called the FBI and reported that I had been kidnapped.

The last time I used my parents' credit card was to purchase six Greyhound tickets. Five of them were diversions. When I got on the bus, I had a jacket, a duffel bag, and about two hundred dollars. I was twenty years old.

The first bus took me from Detroit to Cleveland, a three-hour trip around the western shore of Lake Erie. It wasn't until the bus doors hissed closed behind me in Cleveland that I realized another one wouldn't arrive until the morning. It was a hot summer night, so I wandered through the streets near the bus station looking for a place to rest. I was so tired. My stores of adrenaline had given out. I came across a group of homeless people beginning to settle in for the night. Without much thought, I found a spot on the ground, hugged my duffel bag, and fell into a deep sleep. The sounds of people gathering their belongings in the predawn hours roused me.

I bought a ticket for another unfamiliar place. I stayed on a bus for days, seeing America, my new home, from an oversize grease-smudged window while sitting next to people like me, people running away from something, people with nowhere to go. When one ride ended, I'd buy a couple of Cokes, a couple of Snickers, and another ticket. Sometimes I would see signs for cities I knew the names of, but more often than not, I was lost. I reasoned that if I didn't know where I was no one else could either.

When I remember those long hours, I think of the ache of cold muscles even though it was August. I think of mothers holding babies as they shuffled down the aisle to the foul and claustrophobic bathroom. I think of the man, only trying to be kind, who had pulled my fallen-down jacket back over me as I slept — "Everything is okay; no one is going to hurt you," he said, as I loosened my hands from his neck. I wanted so badly to believe him.

Eventually, I made my way to the mountains of North Carolina where I could hide and work in a friend's aunt's diner. The restaurant belonged to Miss Sara, a Southern Baptist with a Mississippi twang who let me stay in her condo and, in addition to the job, gave me a lesson in American hospitality.

As a Smith graduate, I imagined Miss Sara might want me to manage the Mountaineer or at least run the cash register and say things like "And how was everything today, ma'am?" But when I arrived for my first day of work, Miss Sara led me through the back door past the dumpster and the designated area for smoke breaks. Inside, the kitchen was compact and efficiently arranged. The prep table, the grill, and the heart of the restaurant — the deep fryer. Waitresses and short-order cooks moved around the tight space like a finely tuned orchestra; nobody missed a note as they watched me come in.

We walked directly to the stainless-steel double sink, where a coiled-up industrial faucet swayed from above. Miss Sara shoved the sprayer into my hand and instructed: "Scrape off the food. Hose down the dish. Load it onto this tray. Pull the handle down. Repeat."

Miss Sara was a lot like my grandmother: tough, religious, and cheeky. She cared deeply for her staff and took particular pride in feeding her neighbors. She accepted people as they were. I finally screwed up all of my courage to tell Miss Sara I was gay.

"That's fine, honey," she responded, as she patted my leg. "Just don't be a slut."

As I learned to live on my own in a new country without the support system I once had, I discovered what life is like for many immigrants in America. I was initiated into cultural traditions (moonshine and bacon) and was surprised to find that even this country was full of class divides and racial tension. Mostly, though, I tried on my new role of American, faking my way through "y'all" and "fixin'" and attempting to forge a new life with the weight of the past still tied around my ankle. After my own family rejected me, I found a new one comprised of people few would have expected to welcome a gay Muslim immigrant like me. It was an important lesson. Most people are good; most people want to *do* good.

I also learned how to compartmentalize the past. How to tuck it away and move forward. Most days, I was very good at avoiding painful memories. But that night, on the way home from Shaida's, the stars above me extinguished by the light of the city, I let myself remember.

4

SHIT SHOW

WEEKS AFTER SHAIDA TOLD ME HER FAMILY'S STORY, I was taking Jerome home after practice. He was the youngest of the team, so everyone tended to be protective of him. The boys brought him extra snacks and let him use their bicycles to get back to his apartment complex, which was farther away than everyone else's.

When I looked over at him from the driver's seat, Jerome was holding his stomach.

"What's wrong?" I asked.

"I'm hungry."

"Don't worry about it, you'll be home soon, and you can get something to eat." I wondered if this was a ploy for some fast food.

"No, there is no food at home," he reported matter-of-factly.

"I'm sure there's something? Bread, cheese?"

"No, Coach, it's that time of the month."

I would learn that Jerome meant the time of the month when the food stamps ran out.

I usually walked Jerome to his front door, but that night I walked him inside the apartment. I told him I would help him get some food ready; I expected to find out that he had been exaggerating. Surely there was *something* to eat.

But inside the dark apartment, the cupboards were indeed empty. We found Betty, Jerome's mother, huddled in the corner of the living room, rocking back and forth, shaking her head and muttering, "I work hard every day; every day I work." It was as if she didn't even notice we were there.

I told Jerome to stay there and that I would go get some groceries. On the way to the store, I thought about Betty. I made up a story about her in my head. She probably didn't work enough, or maybe she spent money on things they didn't need.

When I came back to drop off the groceries, the lights were on and Betty greeted me at the door. I couldn't tell if she was angry or grateful to see the bags of food in my hand.

"I don't need this." Her dark eyes were sizing me up. Like Shaida, she looked to be in her forties and wore a colorful housedress. But Betty's posture was different, her body wilted with defeat.

"But Jerome said —"

"I work for my family."

"Ma, this is Coach; she is nice." Jerome was horrified by this tense interaction.

"You know, I also had a hard time when I came to America," I said, trying a different tack.

"You're not American?" Betty said, a hint of warmth in her voice.

"No, I'm from Jordan."

Her face lit up. "You're like us!"

"Kinda, yeah."

Betty told me that she worked at the Ritz-Carlton in Buckhead. She cleaned eighteen rooms a day, and usually that took her twelve hours. She was paid by the room, not the hour, so she didn't earn overtime. Her commute took one hour each way on Atlanta's antiquated public transportation system, otherwise it would have been a twenty-minute drive. She was a single mother with three young boys.

"Jerome talks a lot about you," she said.

"He's a good kid — and a really good player."

"Is he good in school?"

"I think so," I said. It was a guess, but I figured that it was a pretty good guess based on what I knew of Jerome, who was sweet and attentive. "Listen, if there's any way I can help you —"

"Have you met Biko? He's my middle son, he's fourteen. Maybe he can play football, too?"

Soon, a taller, more muscular version of Jerome came out of his room; I had seen him around the field but had never spoken to him.

"This is the coach." Betty pointed at me. "You tell her."

"I want to play," Biko said shyly.

"Well, we only have enough kids for an under-twelve team, Jerome's age."

"How many players do we need for a team?"

I felt uneasy about where this conversation was heading. "Technically, eleven to fourteen, but —"

"Okay. I'll see you tomorrow."

I looked at Betty.

"You can help by coaching my boys." She smiled. Little did I know that this would eventually mean all three of them.

The next day, Biko showed up at the field with more than a dozen boys. Some were older siblings of my under-twelve team, others were kids I had never seen before. They were fourteen and fifteen years old — young men — not the little boys I had been coaching.

At first, the under-twelve team was territorial. The Fugees was their team and this was their time; they didn't want their older siblings around. So I gathered them all up (there were nearly thirty of them now) and explained that I would do my best to coach two teams. One team would start practice at 4 p.m., the other at 5:30, and we would see how it went.

It was one of my under-twelve players, Lewis, who brought Amadou and Mustapha, newly arrived Liberians, to the field. Lewis was my best scout — finding talent but also kids he thought needed a program like ours.

"They are new, Coach," he said. "They love soccer."

Nothing prepared me for Amadou. He was wild and temperamental but sweet and charming at the same time. I tried him out in different positions, and he was good at most of them. He was fast; he had an eye for open spaces and the determination of a freight train.

One day, I asked Amadou to get in goal. He bounded over to it and I threw the goalie gloves to him, which he promptly tossed to the side. Normally, I'd let it slide, but some of these boys had kicks that would leave a bruise the size of a pancake if you didn't move quickly enough. I knew that firsthand, having experienced one of Biko's kicks to my thigh. The bruise lingered for weeks.

I grabbed the gloves from the ground and walked over to Amadou.

"You should put these on," I said, opening one of the gloves for him. He shrugged, and as he slid his right hand into the glove, I noticed that his ring finger was missing, cut off at the second knuckle.

"What happened?" I asked nonchalantly.

"They cut it," he said, just as nonchalantly, and he made a slicing motion with his other hand. Then he laughed and got ready for the shots to come at him.

The first call I ever got from a principal's office was about Amadou. Without telling me, some of the players, including Amadou, had listed my name on their school's emergency contact forms.

"He's fine," the woman from the school told me. "He just had an altercation at school. We need you to come in and pick him up."

"Can you call his mom?"

"She's not answering. Actually, she never answers. Honestly, I'm surprised to get ahold of someone."

"I am at work. Can you explain what happened?"

"As I said, he got in an altercation; we really need you to come in."

I left the café in the hands of one frantic employee and told her I'd be back as soon as possible.

The school was close, and five minutes later, I was in the waiting area of the principal's office. Amadou was sitting in one of the chairs by the door. He gave me a guilty smile when I walked in, clearly relieved that I had shown up.

I put a hand on his shoulder and gave him a once-over. He looked okay. *Why would the principal call me in?* I thought. The kid was fine. I had work.

Then the *other* kid walked out of the office, his mother by his side. He had to be twice Amadou's size, maybe bigger. His nose was swollen, his eyes were swollen, and he was limping. He held an ice pack to his face.

"You're a fucking animal," the mother said to Amadou.

Amadou kept his head down.

"These Africans are animals," she said to me, wanting, I guess, some commiseration, not realizing I was here with the animal she was talking about. At this, Amadou's body stiffened. I put my hand on his chest, found his eyes with mine, and told him to let it go.

He relaxed. Instead, he gave the maimed boy a satisfied smile.

Mother and son left; we could hear them walk down the hall. "How could you let the tiny African beat you up? What kind of man are you . . . ?" The principal emerged from his office.

"Amadou, do you have a family member coming? Should we call her again?"

"This is my coach."

I held out my hand. "Hi, I'm Luma."

He looked confused as he took my hand. "Nice to meet you. You're his . . . ?"

"Coach."

"You know, I can't understand him most of the time." Technically, Amadou spoke English, but he had the animated inflection Liberians are famous for — along with many missing syllables. It's not difficult to understand; you just have to listen carefully.

We sat down and the principal explained what happened. The

boy had made fun of Amadou's stutter, and Amadou had told him to shut up. The boy punched him, so Amadou rearranged his face. It took five teachers to pull him away.

I sat there listening, not sure what I was supposed to do about any of this. Reprimand Amadou?

"Honestly, we've been having a lot of trouble with him since he started. We've sent lots of letters home, and nothing. I'm relieved — and surprised — that you showed up."

"I'll let his mother know what is happening when I see her," I said.

"Can you work on his temper? He's lucky the other family is not pressing charges."

"It won't happen again," I assured the principal, and I felt confident that it wouldn't — who would be foolish enough to pick a fight with Amadou after this?

Back in the car, Amadou, now suspended, was contrite. "I'm sorry, Coach."

"Fighting is not the way to do things," I told him.

"Sometimes you have to fight."

"No. You walk away."

"I am s-s-sorry." Amadou was stuttering; it happened when he got nervous or excited.

"It's fine; I have to go back to work — you know I had to leave work to get you, right? Where is your mom?"

"I don't know, Coach," he said.

The next week, I got another call from the principal.

"We are calling about Amadou. You need to come in and pick him up."

"Can you call his mom?"

"She's not answering."

I sighed. "What did he do this time?"

"I can't really discuss this over the phone."

When I got to the principal's office, Amadou was sitting there with a girl around his age and a woman I guessed to be the girl's mother.

Amadou kept his eyes on the floor as the principal explained that the teenagers had been caught having sex in the bathroom. They were each going to receive a three-day suspension.

A hot rage gathered inside me. As we left the office, I walked three paces ahead of Amadou.

"W-w-where are you going, Coach?" he called after me.

"To work!"

I didn't explain to any of my employees what had happened. For all they knew, Amadou was just a kid on my soccer team earning some pocket change by helping out around the café. He cleaned. He rearranged the giant tubs of ice cream. When it was time for practice, he followed me to my car.

"Nope," I told him before he could get in. "You are going to run. Don't be late." The field was five miles away.

The very next day my phone rang at work. It was Saif, one of my Afghan players. I almost didn't answer. I had committed to coaching these kids — and I was 100 percent committed to doing just that. But I was also 100 percent committed to running a successful business.

"Coach, my mom is in the hospital. She's dying."

"Saif, slow down. What happened?" I said, looking around the café at the people drinking coffee and tapping away on their laptops.

"She took too many pills, and it's all my fault."

It was becoming a routine, leaving work in a frantic rush, driving somewhere unfamiliar, searching for my player-in-distress, and standing there dumbfounded, figuring out what I could do or say to fix the problem.

When I got to Saif's mother's room at the DeKalb Medical Center, he and his sisters were by the bed, their faces wet with tears. I couldn't get a clear explanation about what had happened from any of them. The doctor who came in seemed relieved to find an adult in the room — an English-speaking adult to boot.

Saif's mother was on five medications, a few for her heart, one for blood pressure, another for anxiety. The family had been in the country for less than six months, and none of them could fully understand the instructions printed on each bottle. Saif, trying to help, had given her too many of the wrong pill.

"I killed her," he said. "It's my fault."

"She's not dead," I told him, squeezing his shoulder. I looked at my watch. It was lunch rush at the café.

I stepped out of the room to call the employee I had left in charge. She had predictably — and understandably — had it with me.

"It's going to be a while; there's been an emergency."

"You can't just keep leaving every day; who is going to cover the next shift?" she asked.

I went through my contacts list trying to find someone who could work on short notice. I had no luck. I *couldn't* keep leaving every day, but I couldn't leave the three kids here with their mother on life support. I told myself that I would go in super early the next day. This would be the last emergency.

I took the kids home later that night and picked them up after work the next morning to go back to the hospital. By then, their mother was responsive and out of the ICU. Saif and his sisters were overcome with relief. Later, I took the siblings to the pharmacy, where I bought them a pill box. We went over how to split up the pills at the beginning of each week.

At the next practice, Saif seemed back to normal, but Sein Win, a fifteen-year-old Burmese player, was missing.

"Anyone seen Sein Win?" I asked during warm-ups.

"He's in jail, Coach," someone said casually.

"Jail?"

"Yeah, Coach. He robbed a store yesterday."

It was too much. I needed to blow off some steam. After the café closed Friday night, I locked the doors and brought out the alcohol. Staff stuck around and friends trickled in. We turned up the music and danced. It felt good to be twenty-eight years old again.

Everyone waited for me to pull the plug on the party like I usually did on Fridays. The Fugees played a game most Saturday mornings. But this week I didn't. Every time I would think about the team, I'd pour a shot as if I were playing my own private drinking game. Sein Win in jail — take a shot. Saif's mom on a ventilator — take a shot. Amadou — well, I'd just take a bunch of shots.

The rest of that night is a blur; at some point, the party moved to a bar down the street and I woke up the next morning with a pounding headache and an unfamiliar woman in my bed.

"Where are you going?" she asked groggily, as I rushed around my room collecting my equipment.

"To a game. I have to coach and I'm late."

"Will I see you later?"

"Probably not. Just let yourself out."

At the field, the heat magnified my hangover, and I spent the game sipping Gatorade and hiding behind my cap and sunglasses.

"Are you okay, Coach?" my players asked. They looked worried.

"Yeah, I think I'm just a little sick."

At halftime, I skipped my usual inspirational speech, and in the second half, the team came apart, blaming one another for everything that went wrong. One boy would yell at another boy, then they would both look at me for some kind of a verdict on who was right.

Being their emergency contact was one thing, but now I realized that the boys looked to me for emotional equilibrium, too. It was a responsibility I didn't want. The long estrangement from my family was difficult, but there was a freedom about it that I had gotten used to. I was beholden to nobody.

That night, a couple of the moms called to see if I was feeling better. The boys had told them that I was ill. Did they need to take me to the hospital? Did I need some food?

I wanted to tell them all to just go away. I was practically a kid myself and trying to have some semblance of a social life. Trying to run a café that, if I was honest, was struggling—badly. All I wanted to do was coach a soccer team, and now I had more than two dozen kids on my hands, kids who needed things I couldn't give them.

But they didn't go away. Despite my resistance, they pulled me in further in more complex ways.

The boys began to ask for help with their homework. At first, I was reluctant, but I began helping two or three of them after practice. In addition to coaching in high school, I had been a tutor. Soon, I was tutoring most of the team at the field or in the hallways of their apartment buildings.

For a while, I thought after-school tutoring sessions were helping my players. Many were learning a new language while their parents were working two and three jobs. I assumed that I could fill in the gap not covered by school or family. I was so naive.

Like many of my players, Lewis was having trouble in school. Three years before I met him, Lewis and his family were forced to leave their home in Wau, South Sudan, to escape one of the most brutal and deadliest civil wars in history. He had missed years of schooling; it made sense that he needed a tutor.

I was sitting with Lewis on a park bench near the field one day, helping him with a worksheet.

"Read it to me, Coach," he said. "I have a headache." So I read to him, then asked the worksheet's questions aloud. He answered each one correctly.

The next week, Lewis complained of another headache. Again, I read aloud.

The third week, Lewis complained of yet another headache.

"That's funny," I said. "I have a headache, too."

"You do, Coach?"

"I do. So this week you can read to me."

After a few seconds of silence (that felt like twenty minutes), Lewis looked up at me. I will never forget the shame and dejection in his eyes as he said, "I can't read."

Lewis had successfully advanced three grades in an American school by the time he told me that he couldn't read.

Everything started making sense. Saif misinterpreting the medication. Amadou acting out in school. Sein Win getting arrested. Jerome's family not having enough food.

There were two Americas, I could see now, one for those who have access to opportunity and one for those who never will. An America where parents don't have to worry about feeding their children and an America where a woman who cleans eighteen hotel rooms a day cannot provide for hers. An America where the kids thrive in their schools and an America where the kids get bullied, abandoned, left behind.

Where was the America that had taken me in? That had protected me? That had embraced me? That had allowed me to build myself back up? How could I get my players to *that* America?

5

A MORE CONVENIENT SEASON

I DON'T KNOW WHAT I WAS WAITING FOR, MAYBE A LOOK OF surprise or shock? Outrage would have been good. Instead, the woman in front of me — lips pursed, eyes blank — appeared almost bored by what I was telling her: my twelve-year-old player, her student, could not read.

"That happens. A lot of kids can't read in his class."

Shocked by her reaction, I stammered, "Well, I mean, what should I do? This can't be acceptable?"

"I'm not sure there's anything you *can* do." She gave me a smile meant to punctuate the conversation.

"So I should just accept that he can't read? That's what you're saying?"

"I'm saying Lewis is a really good kid. He's kind; he doesn't get in trouble. He's better off than so many of them. He'll be okay."

I thought I knew American schools. The school run by the American embassy in Amman was like this one, filled with kids from all over the world. In the cafeteria, we traded the lunches our parents had packed: sushi for curry for hummus. Academics were rigorous, but so were the arts and athletic programs. All of my classmates went on to elite colleges.

Weren't all schools in America like the one I had attended in Jordan? It didn't take more than two minutes with Lewis's teacher to realize that, in fact, they weren't.

I called an old friend from Smith, a teacher. She explained that the richer and whiter a district was, the better the schools generally were.

I was confused. "Why?"

"The students don't have to deal with some of the stuff poor kids deal with. And also the school gets more money."

"Why?"

"Because schools get money from local property taxes."

"In Georgia?"

"Everywhere."

"Schools don't get the same amount of money? How is that fair? I thought everyone was entitled to a free and excellent education." Somewhere along the line, maybe in college, I had learned about the Rehabilitation Act of 1973, which guaranteed education to all students regardless of their learning disabilities.

"No, they are entitled to a free and *appropriate* education," my friend corrected me.

Apparently, I had misremembered the word. Not excellent, appropriate. What did that even mean?

I thought of seeing my students high-fiving Jean Claude, a recent arrival from Burundi.

"What are we celebrating?" I had asked.

"Jean Claude can leave the International Center! He knows English!"

I felt my brow furrow. Jean Claude had been in Georgia for barely six months; he had trouble piecing together an entire sentence, often slipping back into Kirundi when he'd get stuck. The boys had seen my skepticism and tried to explain.

"The International Center is a place where you go when you first get here, then they let you out."

Their vague description made me even more curious. "Is it a school?"

The boys looked at one another. "Not really."

"Do you go all day?"

"Yes."

"Do you take classes?"

"Yes."

"And when do you get out?"

"When they think you can go to the regular school."

"A few years?"

"A few months."

Remarkably, the boys were right. Jean Claude had enrolled at the International Student Center, a newcomer center in our county. These programs were designed for recent immigrants who have little or no English proficiency and limited formal education. I would learn that there were very few standard requirements for students at newcomer centers. Some states mandated six months, others said that in "extreme cases" students could stay for a year. Mostly, the system seemed set up to rush kids through, to mainstream them into general education classrooms as soon as possible. This was true especially for older students, who are expected to meet all the high school requirements in a new language, be college ready, and achieve the same outcomes in the same amount of time as their native-born peers.

It seemed like such a missed opportunity. My limited time with the Fugees had demonstrated that the kids desperately needed focused attention. Maybe Lewis would have learned to read if he'd been given more time in a stable, supportive environment when he first arrived.

Jean Claude would be joining Amadou at the middle school where I was well acquainted with the principal's office, thanks to Amadou, and where, as it happened, I would be sitting in on a class the next day.

From the back of their classroom, I was able to see both of my players. The scene was chaotic; the teacher had to yell to be heard over the roar of the students' conversation.

Jean Claude sat stiffly in his seat, his best impression of a smile glued to his face. He watched the other kids, mimicking their mannerisms and gestures.

"Okay, everybody; we've got a new student."

Jean Claude's spine straightened.

"Jean Claude," the teacher said. All eyes turned to Jean Claude.

"Yes."

"Welcome. Do you like school?"

"Yes."

"And where did you come from?"

"Yes."

The class erupted into giggles. Beneath his desk, Jean Claude clutched the hem of his shirt, that smile still stuck in place. He had been born and raised in a refugee camp in Tanzania; I knew Jean Claude was resilient. But it broke my heart to see that resilience tested here in what should have been a safe place.

The teacher quickly moved on to the next item on the agenda.

This happened over and over again. I visited nearly every middle school my players attended, and every time I witnessed the same thing. A classroom crammed with thirty kids, a teacher struggling to maintain order. Students walking in and walking out, a few in the front doing their best to pay attention.

I would leave each school with a splitting headache.

I began to believe the answer for my students was to get them in better schools. I started googling "good schools Atlanta." I learned that there was a more affluent district north of us and some promising private schools, too.

I made an appointment with the admissions officer at a private school that was considered to be one of the best in the state. I let her think that I had a child of my own to enroll.

We sat and spoke for an hour; she told me about LEED-certi-fied buildings, the Model UN, the birding club, the annual science carnival. She took me on a tour of the leafy campus, and we observed classes where students sat, quiet and attentive. It was seven miles and a world away from what my players experienced at their schools. As I walked around, I wondered if they would feel more welcome here.

"So what do you do for non-English speakers?" I asked.

"As in . . . no English?"

"New to the country."

"It depends on how young they are. If they are kindergarten or first grade, it could still be a fit." She looked confused now, trying to sort out if I was an adoptive parent or new to the country myself.

"Well, academically, they are kindergarten or first grade . . ." I decided not to finish my thought.

"Oh! We *did* have great success with a Bosnian student!" She gave me a satisfied grin. "He was Bosnian and went through the war and just added so much to our school."

If this mysterious Bosnian kid could do it, I thought that some of my players surely could.

"Of course, they would still need to take the admissions exam, but I am sure your child would do well."

At the end of our time together, she presented me with an application and the tuition schedule. The tuition was more — a lot more — than many of my players' parents earned in one year.

Hopeful that maybe I could tackle the test part first and the money part second, I pulled aside a few of my players who I thought were the strongest academically. I told them about the school and how I thought they might be a good fit.

"You'd have to take a test."

"What kind of a test?"

"Probably a reading and writing test. Maybe a math test."

"Why?"

"So they can see . . ." I couldn't bring myself to finish the sentence with *if you're smart enough*. In that moment, I realized how silly I was being. Those tests would never tell the admissions counselor how smart my players were.

My players were stuck between two bad options. The private schools in the area didn't need to and simply didn't admit under-prepared students. They might take one or two of the top performers, kids who would likely succeed in any school, if only to spotlight them in fundraising campaigns or tout them to prospective parents. And there were public schools, institutions that accepted everyone, but that were, in the districts where the Fugees lived, haphazardly funded and ill-equipped to address the needs of English-language learners, whose traumatic backgrounds had left them far behind their grade levels.

It didn't seem that complicated — my players needed a school committed to making sure *every* student felt safe and accepted, and received the attention and skills required to succeed, with well-trained teachers prepared to make that happen. They shouldn't have to move to a different neighborhood or take an admission test to find it. No kid should.

Halfway through that first summer, the YMCA reached out to say that they were sending a photographer to the field to get some shots of the team as we practiced. I had been coaching for four years and had never received such a request.

Not long afterward, I noticed that the YMCA was using those photos prominently on its website. Sulayman's monster smile, Amadou looking serious in goal, the posed shot of us together, me surrounded by six beaming boys. They were using our story to support their annual fundraising campaign.

The next surprise came when I learned that I had been chosen as the volunteer of the year for the Decatur/DeKalb branch of the Atlanta YMCA. Volunteer of the year? I knew many other people in the neighborhood who had done much more and for longer than I had. Regardless, I would need to come in to film an interview, and the team was invited to the annual black-tie dinner at the Hyatt Regency in downtown Atlanta, a skyscraper with a rotating restaurant on top. There would be a table reserved just for us. I couldn't fit more than four kids in my car, so I asked the YMCA if we could borrow a bus. They agreed.

Growing up, I had attended several charity events with my family in Jordan. I hated them. Hated getting dressed up, hated watching people congratulate themselves for helping others. If they really wanted to help, why not take all the money they spent on makeup and clothes and champagne, and give it to the people who needed it? It all felt empty to me. Still, I didn't want to seem ungrateful. I felt obligated to go.

I still had the suit my mom had bought me when she dropped me off at college almost a decade earlier. (She was right: a pinstripe Ralph Lauren suit lasts a lifetime.) I was more concerned about what the kids would wear. Asking for the bus was one thing, but asking for a clothes budget was another. Even though we needed it. Instead, I drove to the thrift store and filled a shopping cart with dark pants, collared shirts, and ties.

At our next practice, I told them we were getting an award.

"Are you winning a trophy, Coach?"

"I don't think so, maybe."

I told them they would have to dress up.

"Can we wear tennis shoes?"

"No, dress shoes."

"Dress shoes?"

"Church shoes."

"Oh, church shoes."

An employee at the café, a woman named Ebony, offered to help chauffeur and chaperone the kids; we retrieved them one by one from their apartments. We didn't want them to get their clothes dirty on their way to the bus.

Downtown, Peachtree Street was crowded and hot; walking into the gilded atrium of the Hyatt Regency was like entering another dimension. Every surface was glass or marble or crystal. The kids' eyes were as wide as dinner plates as they watched the elevators climb skyward. Seeing the hotel through their eyes made it seem fabulously ornate, like a Roald Dahl book come to life.

One of the boys said to another: "I think my mom works here. I know it's a hotel downtown."

We found our way to the ballroom where the dinner would be held. As we walked to our table, the boys nervously tucked and re-tucked their shirts and smoothed their hair with the palms of their hands. Looking around, I noticed that we were in the presence of Atlanta's beautiful and powerful. My players were the only kids at the dinner.

"Why are there so many forks, Coach?" they asked, when we were seated.

"Because we are going to eat a lot!" I said, trying to replace their apprehension with excitement.

"We will eat two chickens!" one boy yelled.

"And two goats!" said another.

But then another asked: "Why do we need the forks? Can't we just eat with our hands?"

My heart dropped. I had been so focused on all the parts of this that made *me* uncomfortable — the dressing up, the haircuts — that I had completely forgotten what might make *them* uncomfortable. Many of the boys came from countries where eating with your hands was the norm.

"Okay, guys, listen up. Some people eat differently. For dinner, just copy what I do. Whatever I do, just do that." They nodded in agreement.

The food arrived and I placed my napkin on my lap. They placed napkins on their laps, too. The salad arrived and I conspicuously picked up the small outer fork. The boys picked up that fork, too.

I noticed that one boy was simply poking at the greens, moving them around his plate.

"If you don't want to eat it, you don't have to," I reassured him. "Just put your fork on the plate and they will take it away."

"What will they do with it?"

"Probably just throw it away."

Every salad plate was squeaky-clean by the time the server came back to get them.

When the main course came out, I watched as the boys struggled clumsily with their knives and forks, obviously frustrated. The utensils slipped through their small hands; they fell with a clatter onto their plates.

"Hey, guys?" I said, and they all looked up at me. I put down my own utensils, tore off a piece of chicken with my fingers, and dipped it in the mashed potatoes. They smiled, abandoned their forks and knives, and dug in.

After dinner, when the server asked if I would like coffee, I said, "Yes, please," and all of the boys said, "Yes, please," too. Their first coffees, at 9 p.m. on a weeknight. Their mothers would be thrilled.

The awards ceremony began. The room went dark and the screen above the stage lit up with our faces and footage of the boys playing soccer barefoot in jean shorts and secondhand shirts. The interview I had recorded played over the montage. Hearing it now, I was horrified to realize that I had told some of the boys' stories—the sad and brutal parts—without their permission. I also realized that the interviewer hadn't even asked me anything about *soccer*, about the boys' performance or their strengths, or even how a team sport was helping them work through their trauma. Ebony looked at me from across the table. I knew what she was thinking.

I sank low in my seat, embarrassed and angry. I thought about a word I had learned in college: "ethnoporn." I hadn't quite understood it then, but I did now.

It was difficult to gauge the boys' reaction. They tugged at their ties and looked confused, not relating to the story that was being told about them. Maybe they hoped some part of tonight would be about them as players instead of them as helpless refugees.

After the program, people filed out, many stopping to compliment or thank me about what I was "doing for these kids." *These kids*, I thought. As if *these kids* were somehow essentially different from their kids.

On the way out, the director of the YMCA patted my shoulder. "Thank you for putting us on the map!" He grinned. I said something about needing to get the boys home and herded the Fugees to the door.

"Guys, I'm sorry," I said, once we were all seated on the bus.

"For what, Coach?"

"For bringing you here."

I made it up to them with Krispy Kreme, where we sat beneath the glow of fluorescent lights, ties loosened and jackets thrown off, licking the glaze from our fingers.

I knew that what I was giving my players — the chance to be a part of a team, to have supportive relationships with other refugees like themselves — was valuable. But I couldn't stop feeling that for many of them this was *it*. After they aged out of youth soccer, what was next for them? A dead-end job? A crappy apartment? I didn't want to see them peak at age twelve.

I had one last idea. A couple of my players went to a K–5 charter school in Decatur with an enrollment split between native-born and foreign-born students. Sidi and Patrick seemed to be excelling there — not academically but socially. It was a start. When I learned that the school was considering expanding to serve middle and high school students, I scheduled a meeting with one of the board members. They were experts in opening a school and I was an up-and-coming community organizer. Maybe we could work something out together.

We met at a coffee shop across the street from the school on a very bright morning. This woman was probably twice my age, small in stature with graying brown hair.

"Right now, we haven't made a decision one way or the other," she said. "We're forming a committee to explore our options."

"How often does the committee meet? Maybe I could explain the situation and the needs of the community?"

"I'll have to let you know," she said. It wasn't the first evasive answer she had given me.

I asked, "In the meantime, what will happen to your students who finish fifth grade next year, like Patrick and Sidi?"

"They will go to their home school, the school they were zoned for." She meant the chaotic classrooms I had been visiting for weeks. What she didn't say was that most of the native-born students were zoned for excellent schools. The ones who weren't would be attending private schools.

I knew she was on the defensive, but I was desperate. I needed an ally.

"I think there should be a school for kids like my players, who are older when they arrive. A place where they can be taught at their level, learn about who they are, and learn about their new home."

"You mean a school *only* for them."

"Yes."

"Don't you think integration should be the goal?"

"They are not ready to integrate."

"So, what you're suggesting is . . . segregation." She said it as if it were a curse word.

"I didn't say that."

"If it's only for them, then that's segregation."

"Okay, fine. Sure — call it segregation. But for my kids to successfully integrate, maybe they need to be segregated for a time so they can heal and learn without being made fun of and not just get put on a conveyor belt through the system. What we're doing isn't working."

"Well, our school *integrates*. It's based on MLK's Beloved Community."

"So do your refugee students perform at the same level as your native-born kids?"

"You can't expect them to. Besides, we also consider what our American students are getting out of the experience."

"I don't care what they are getting; I want to know what *we* are getting."

The conversation was getting heated. She knew my reputation was strong, that my influence was growing, that families trusted me. Maybe she wasn't used to being challenged.

"Have you ever heard of Idi Amin?"

That's when I left. The only thing Idi Amin and I had in common was that we were both Muslim.

I still don't know if it was a dig at my Arabness or my approach, but it was only the beginning of the pushback I would encounter.

On the field, picking out the racists was easy. They were the people who hissed the slurs, shot the dirty looks. Those people didn't bother me. At least they didn't try to hide their bigotry behind the guise of some progressive cause designed with only the good feeling of the giver in mind, not the dignity of the receiver.

What everyone wanted from us, I was beginning to realize, was to shut up and play soccer. To be the feel-good story they could point to and say: "*See*, refugees can make it here." My players were allowed this one success story but not another. They could be feted at a black-tie dinner, but they would never be the ones throwing it. We could be the anomaly in the system, but we could not ask to change the system.

Ultimately, regardless of how talented my players were, they could go only so far.

The board member had evoked MLK's concept of "beloved community." Maybe that's what made me think of another MLK quote, this one from "Letter from Birmingham Jail," where he outlines his grave disappointment with the "white moderate" who always says: "'I agree with you in the goal you seek, but I can't agree with your methods of direct action'; who paternalistically feels he can set the timetable for another man's freedom . . . who constantly advises the Negro to wait until a 'more convenient season.'"

We couldn't wait for a more convenient season. The Fugees needed change now.

6

IMAGINE

WELL-INTENTIONED PEOPLE OFTEN ASK ME TO TELL them about the refugee experience. For many reasons, this is an impossible request to answer. Every refugee experience is different. Shaida and her boys endured years of direct physical threats and danger. While my asylum process unfolded mostly in law offices, I suffered from severe anxiety, mood swings, and nightmares so real that I would wake up screaming. While Shaida and I share similar scars, our stories are very different.

Although we often pass around the old cliché about walking in someone else's shoes, we usually can't. Our imagination will always be limited by our own assumptions, politics, and cultural blind spots, not to mention our built-in instinct to avoid things that upset us or make us feel guilty. Sure, we might be able to sit through a news segment about the latest spate of bombings or watch a documentary about life in a refugee camp, but at the end of the day, we walk in our own shoes.

Unfortunately, it's becoming even more important for those of us living in Western democracies to begin to truly *feel* — not just understand — this crisis. There are more than eighty million refugees in the world, the highest number in recorded history. Half of them are children. One person is displaced every three seconds, and by the time you finish reading this sentence, at least five people will have been displaced. By the time you finish reading this book, approximately 9,600 people will have been forced to leave their homes for good. By 2050, there will be an estimated 1.2 billion refugees in the world as climate change makes parts of the globe uninhabitable.

I know that these statistics are numbing. I know that for people to care they need stories. That's why they ask about the refugee experience. But stories about other people go only so far. Maybe you already have seen photos of Kabul on the news and can picture Shaida in that market with her young son. But can you *feel* it? Probably not. You live in a democracy. You post your political opinions online without fear of going to jail and being tortured. You don't fall asleep at night to the sound of bombs. Short of placing you in a simulation so you can feel your own heart knock against your chest as you flee your home, stories are all we have. So, instead of shoes, let's put you in this story.

Imagine you are living in Ohio. During the past few weeks, small skirmishes have broken out at the border of Ohio and Indiana. There's always been tension, both states battling it out to be the dominant political force in the Midwest; but for the most part, any violence has been isolated and brief, carried out by people you consider extremists. Even though the news says things are escalating, you don't worry *too* much about it. You're not really a political person, and you have faith that the government will squash the fighting soon.

But then you see your next-door neighbor packing up her SUV with as many belongings as she can fit in. She tells you that she thinks the violence will continue; she knows people near the fighting, and they say things are different this time. She's taking her family to Pennsylvania to be safe. The conversation shakes you, but you think your neighbor is blowing things out of proportion. Every now and then, on cloudy nights, you can hear the bombs, but you will wait it out. Your home is where you feel safest. Any day now, you think, this thing will be over.

Weeks go by. One afternoon, on your way home from work, a thick gray smoke makes it hard to see the road. Not only can you hear the bombs, you can see their flashes, too. Sirens are going off and every radio station is blaring evacuation messages, much like they do when a severe storm is imminent or an Amber Alert is issued. When you pull onto your street, you are startled to see many of your neighbors walking away in groups, backpacks and blankets and diaper bags slung around their bodies. An acquaintance you remember from last year's block party waves you down. He says the Indiana army is moving in. They have already bombed the airport and the interstates. All the major bridges are out. Word has it that they are thirty minutes away from the neighborhood. Everyone is walking to Kentucky, hoping the camp that has been set up for evacuees is still taking people in. "Get your children," he says. "And get out. Hurry."

When you step inside your front door, you frantically take stock.

What do you take?

What food should you pack? How much of it?

How many water bottles should you fill?

What about your laptop? Where will you charge it?

Do you need cash? Do you have any at home?

Should you find the birth certificates? Where is your passport? Has it expired?

You do some quick math in your head. Kentucky is 147 miles away. If you can keep everyone moving at three miles per hour, you might be able to do that in . . . fifty hours?

What shoes should you wear?

Should you bring extra socks?

A sleeping bag?

Can you carry enough food and water *and* sleeping bags for everyone?

Who should you call?

Your parents? Your sister?

Should you call work to let them know that you won't be in for . . . a while?

Of course not. No one will be there.

You look around the room at the framed portraits of your kids. The art you've collected. Everything that makes your home your home. You know that you can't take any of that, but you spend precious seconds trying to figure out how you can. You have a bad feeling that whatever you leave behind you will never see again. Never.

What about the jewelry?

Is it safe to carry valuables?

Your partner is shouting, telling the kids to hurry up. To get gym shoes on. All three of them are under ten, but at least the youngest one can walk. But can he walk three miles an hour? He can't, of course. So you'll have to carry him. But can you carry him and the sleeping bags at the same time?

Don't panic.

Breathe.

You will keep them safe.

A bomb explodes. It's so close that you can feel the reverberations in the soles of your shoes. Another bomb explodes. Was that one closer? Your partner is trying to speak calmly to the children, but you recognize the panic in their voice. "Let's go, let's go."

"What about the dog?" your youngest asks. You fill the bowl with all the dog food you have left. You fill two buckets with water. You leave the back door open. "The dog will be fine," you tell him. *The dog will be fine*, you tell yourself.

Your phone is buzzing like crazy in your pocket. Your sister wants to know where you are. Friends are reporting their routes. The phone rings. It's your parents.

You stare at the screen.

Do you have a portable phone charger?

One hundred and forty-seven miles. Fifty hours.

You take one more look around. Books. Plants. Pictures. Your coffee maker.

As soon as you walk out the front door, you realize, heart thudding, that you took too long to leave. The military is here. There is a scuffle, then a stampede, then shooting and smoke. You close your eyes to keep out the smoke and the dust and the sight of people being hurt. You hold on to the straps of your children's backpacks. You tell them to walk. "Walk. Don't stop." You cut through some backyards to another street the soldiers haven't gotten to yet. The kids are in front of you, but when you look to your side, your partner is gone. You look behind you. Fat clouds of smoke are rising over your beautiful neighborhood. You can't go back there with the children. You can't leave them.

Don't panic.

Don't scream.

Breathe.

You said you'd meet up at the camp if you got separated. So you stick to the plan. The plan is all you have. Not ten minutes later, the youngest is crying. He's scared, his feet hurt, he wants to be carried. The other kids carry two sleeping bags apiece and you carry the toddler.

You pass an ATM machine. There is no line. You remember you need cash. You have only $63 on you. You put your card in. You type in your PIN. You request $800. The machine beeps and the screen says, *Insufficient funds to complete your transaction.* You know there is more than $800 in your account. You request $600. *Insufficient funds to complete your transaction.* The dread is rising in your throat. $200. *Insufficient funds to complete your transaction.* You hit cancel.

The screen goes black. It doesn't return your card. You press all the buttons. You kick the machine. You want to scream. Your kids are watching you. The crowd is moving. You must keep walking.

An hour later, the sun is setting, and the kids are looking tired. The ache in your lower back says you packed too much.

What do you leave behind?

How do you ration the food and water?

The crowd swells, but that doesn't comfort you. Will there be room for everyone at the camp? Parents are carrying their children. Their pets. An old man is pushing an old woman in a wheelchair. It is getting dark. It starts getting cold. Groups of people stop walking, wanting to rest for the evening. They huddle together. They make some fires to stay warm.

The man behind you says, "Don't stop, keep going, they are right behind us. Everyone who stays here will be killed." He offers to carry a bag. The bag with the food and the birth certificates.

You look at him.

Do you give him the bag?

Why is he alone?

Why isn't he carrying anything himself?

You grip the bag tighter and shake your head no. He shrugs and walks ahead. You begin to slow down. More and more people are stopping to rest for the night. The kids are whimpering. You see an open grassy area next to another family and drop your things as if they were an anchor. You pull out a bag of food and hand an apple to each one of your kids. The family next to you is staring. They don't have any food. The mother looks at you, her eyes kind but desperate.

"We've been walking for three days; we just have to keep going," she says. Is she talking to you or herself?

You have two more apples, four bananas, and six granola bars.

You give them an apple, a banana, and a granola bar. The two kids share the apple. The mother stuffs the rest in her pocket.

"Thank you," she says. You wonder if you have made a mistake. You wonder if this is really happening.

You use your body to cover your belongings; the four of you cuddle together under the two sleeping bags you have left after having decided to jettison the other two along the way. The kids shiver. They don't complain. You layer them in their clothes.

Too tense to sleep, you text your partner. No response. You text your mom. No response. You text your sister. No response. Are the texts even going through? You check the news. The army is ransacking each town it comes to. Killing people indiscriminately. Kids are being taken away from their parents. Pennsylvania has sealed its border. Kentucky is being inundated. There is a site with a list of names of those who have been taken in by the Ohio government for questioning. You scour the list to search for your partner, for your parents, for anyone you know. You don't recognize any of the names.

You log in to your bank accounts. Your account balance is $0. $0 for checking. $0 for savings. $0 for retirement. You google "bank account zero." All bank accounts in Ohio have been seized by the government.

You finally fall asleep.

You are shaken awake by the mother next to you. It's still dark. "We have to go before they get here." You wake up your kids. Everyone is tired and confused and cold. You brush your teeth without water.

You pack your stuff. Check your phone. No messages. You start walking. You pass a sign that says, KENTUCKY: 135 MILES.

You walk for days. Your feet throb. Everything hurts. You hear from no one in your family. Each night, you scour the lists for names you recognize. Nothing. On the fourth night, you don't know if you can go on. As you settle in, someone starts yelling, "Come for food; come for water." There is a relief group distributing food and water. You become hopeful: if you can eat and drink, you can make it through the last two days. You round up your kids to follow the crowd.

The woman you shared your food with tugs on your hand, and says, "Don't go." You're confused. How can you not go? Not feed your children? You pull away. She says, "They will kill you."

Do you believe her?

Would she have warned you if you hadn't given her the apple?

You stay. Your phone battery is low. The portable charger is done. There are no power outlets anywhere.

You hear rapid gunshots in the distance. Then more. The woman looks at you. Your eyes meet. You clutch your children for a long, long time, pushing your nose into their unwashed hair.

You walk until, finally, you pass a sign. KENTUCKY WELCOMES YOU.

A mile later, you see the line. Hundreds — thousands? — of people lining up to get in. There's barbed wire in the distance.

You wait. And wait. And wait. You reach the front of the line.

You give your name and your children's names. You provide your ID and birth certificates. You start to ask questions as quickly as you can. Instead of answers, you are given two blankets and pointed toward the direction of the fenced-in camp.

Kentucky doesn't want you. The state has its own problems. It wants to stay out of the military conflict, which is unpopular with voters. It is an election year. So you will stay on the border in this fenced-in encampment with your three children and these two blankets. The next day, you are assigned a tent not much larger than the one your family used for camping trips. You are told food is distributed every day at 11 a.m.

Every day you line up. Sometimes you are given bread. Sometimes it's rice or lentils. Once a week, you're handed a can of tuna.

Three weeks in, your kids stop asking when they are going home.

They know. You know. You have seen the pictures of your neighborhood completely destroyed. Looted and bombed. There is nothing left.

Four months in, your kids stop asking about their grandparents. They know. You know. You have seen the names of the elderly who could not get out. Your mom's name right after your dad's. Abandoned and buried in mass graves. They are gone.

A year in, your kids stop asking about your partner, their parent, your rock, the love of your life. They know. You know. You have seen the videos of the mass execution in the football stadium. Murdered and executed and all alone. Their blood staining the grass. They are dead.

Somehow, this becomes normal. Food only once a day, water only in bottles. No work, no school. You sit on old sleeping bags and mattresses and talk to other people about nothing. There is nothing to talk about. Nothing to think about. Nothing to dream about.

For two years, you apply to get out. To be resettled into another, safer country. You know this is like buying a dollar scratch-off and winning a million dollars. But you do it anyway. Every once in a while, you and your children are taken to UN tents. Your children are taken from you and separated from one another. They are all asked the same questions. Names. Birthdays. Home address. When did you leave? Were you tortured? Are you involved in a political party? Did you support the governor? Where is your partner? Where is your parent? How do you know they are dead? They repeat the questions over and over. The interviewers try to catch you in a lie. If one of you contradicts the other in even the tiniest detail, you will be denied resettlement. You wait.

And then one day you see your name on the resettlement list. You are getting out. Your family is one of five families selected that month to leave the camp and start a new life in China. Your family is one of tens of thousands of families waiting for the same news.

China takes in five families a year. One of the richest countries in the world takes in five families out of the eleven thousand that have been displaced. You feel sick with relief and guilt.

The next day, you board a plane. Fourteen hours later, you land in China. A man is there to greet you. He holds a board with your name written on it. But he knows who you are. You are the ones who don't look like anyone else. You are the ones who look bewildered and lost.

He speaks to you in Mandarin. No one in your family understands Mandarin. He smiles. You smile. Is this the first real smile you have smiled in two years? You still have that one bag with the birth certificates. You still have your children.

You get in his car and he takes you to a run-down apartment. It is dark when you arrive. The apartment has two mattresses on the floor, a TV, and unfamiliar groceries on the table. The man gives you a box with warm food in it. He points to his watch and says something you don't understand and leaves.

Soon, you will go to work cleaning office buildings. No one cares about your master's degree, and the bill for your flight to China will need to be repaid. Your children will go to school where they look different from everyone else and where no one is prepared to educate them. People you pass on the street will eye you suspiciously. Sometimes people will tell you to go back to where you came from and you will think, *If only*.

But now you sit on the floor with your children. You open the box of food. You have no idea what it is. You look at one another and laugh. You eat every last bite. You are safe. You are alive. You are lucky.

For more than eighty million people (six times the population of the entire state of Ohio), this story is not hypothetical. For them, the haunting hypothetical is whether they will be resettled and given the chance to start a new life.

Who gets chosen? Who is approved? As hard as it is to believe, the future of eighty million refugees and asylum seekers is decided by sheer and utter luck. Instead of an intentional, compassionate system, it is one that is designed to say no. A system that assumes victims of war and atrocities are liars. A system that required Shaida to prove that her husband was killed and that her life was in danger even though the world's media was saturated with stories detailing the cruelty and lawlessness of the Taliban.

I was lucky. I could afford an experienced lawyer who did not have an overwhelming caseload. I had a dedicated research team in my Smith College classmates, and I speak English fluently. I was prepped for the interview. But nothing could prepare me for the antagonizing questions, the insinuation that I had dishonest intentions. I had to prove that I was gay. The CIA profile on Jordan was accessible to the officer, but *I* had to provide it. I had to relive my trauma. After hours of this, I lost my temper. "Why would anyone make this up?" I asked. "Do you understand that I will no longer have a home? I will no longer have a family?" I stormed out of my own hearing.

The Refugee Act of 1980 was signed into law by President Jimmy Carter in response to this lack of a clear and fair process for refugee admissions. The new legislation gave the president the ability to adjust admission numbers based on the prevalence of international conflict and humanitarian crises. But the law failed to implement a logical, mathematical method for deciding those numbers based on need. Instead, the number of refugees the United States takes in every year is largely arbitrary. Most often, the figure is based on what is politically convenient. For instance, after the Iraq War, Iraqis were fast-tracked because many had assisted the US military by providing much-needed translation services. During the War in Afghanistan, Afghans were allowed in in greater numbers, perhaps to snuff out growing public opposition to the conflict. After President Obama issued his "red line" comment, then walked back from it despite the

Assad regime's use of chemical warfare, which killed 1,500 civilians, he earmarked resettlement for ten thousand Syrians. That may seem generous until you realize that eleven million Syrians were forced to leave their homes through no fault of their own.

Still, for many decades, the United States led the world in refugee admissions, admitting more than all other countries combined in some years. During the Trump administration, though, that number plummeted. Only eleven thousand refugees were resettled in America in 2020. Even with these historically low figures, xenophobia and antirefugee sentiments have intensified, exacerbated by politicians who use other people's suffering to encourage fear and nativism.

We desperately need a fair and transparent policy to determine refugee admissions. We need consistent systems in place to allow for smoother adjustment to life in the United States. What if our refugee admissions number was tied to a percentage of the number of refugees globally? What if our resettlement process engaged Americans in sponsoring, teaching, and welcoming refugees to their new home? What if we were all lucky enough to have a Miss Sara or a Shaida (and her incredible cooking) in our lives? We could help her understand what it means to be an American, and she could help us understand the impact our foreign policy has on real people around the world so we might be more informed voters and have a hand in strengthening America's position in the world.

And what if refugees got a seat at the table to help design policies that affect them? What if — instead of infantilizing and dehumanizing these new Americans — we asked for their help to create a fairer and more just system?

It's vital for us to remember that refugees are not simply another category of immigrants. They did not *choose* to leave their homes, did not *choose* to be victimized and traumatized, and did not *choose* to have their fortunes forever yoked to the political whims of a foreign country.

No other country in the world claims to have the values that America has championed from its very founding. We say that we are proud to be a melting pot of the tired, the poor, the homeless, and the tempest-tossed. But as long as we continue to turn a blind eye to the huddled masses at our door, it's not their humanity we're betraying, it's our own.

7

SHOO BAIDEIN?

B Y 2006, MY ROSTER OF FUGEES CONSISTED OF THREE teams and about sixty boys. As our ranks expanded, so did our needs. We needed uniforms, cleats, shin guards, water bottles, and soccer balls. Sometimes friends sent personal checks to support the cause, but I was always on the hunt for a bargain and often paying for things out of my own pocket.

We were still playing in the YMCA league, which meant I couldn't apply for the majority of youth sports grants since technically we had a sponsoring body. There was one US Soccer Foundation grant we qualified for, and I spent many evenings poring over the application. Eventually, we were awarded ten thousand dollars to spend on equipment and uniforms. We had always played in a ragtag mix of green and yellow (an homage to Brazil, my favorite national team), but that year the Fugees took the field in construction-barrel-orange jerseys — because they were the only ones on sale.

It was becoming apparent that we needed more support than a smattering of private donations and random grants. And so I did what any serious social entrepreneur does ... I went to the bookstore and bought *The Nonprofit Kit for Dummies,* the one that came with a CD-ROM that would walk me through the process of becoming a nonprofit step by step.

The first thing I needed for the nonprofit—the first blank right there at the top of the page — was a name. I thought back to a conversation I had recently had with Jerome, aka One Shoe. It was Christmas time, and I mentioned to the boys that I would be heading to Massachusetts for the holiday to visit my best friend, Misty. That day when I stopped to drop Jerome off at his apartment after practice, he lingered in the passenger's seat quietly. Finally, he turned to me with tears in his eyes, and said, "What's going to happen to the Fugees family?"

"What do you mean?" I asked.

"You're leaving and you're never coming back."

"I didn't say I was *leaving*. I said I am going on vacation and that I will be back."

He didn't seem satisfied with the answer. I tried to explain what a vacation was, that I was tired and needed a break. But that wasn't the right approach either. I said I missed my friend and really wanted to see her and her family. A little better but not quite right.

"Listen, I am coming back, and we will play soccer again." I thought quickly for some way I could convince Jerome not to worry. "You know I never go anywhere without my watch, right? So why don't you keep my watch until I come back, okay?"

I peeled off my bright orange Swatch and handed it to Jerome, who wrapped it around his arm with a satisfied look.

Each day during my week in New England, I got a call from Jerome, who couldn't read my analog watch. "Coach, what time is it?" he asked.

Until that moment in the car with Jerome, I had thought of us as a team, but I realized that we weren't just a team, we were a *family*. The Fugees Family. So that is what I wrote on that first line.

The next thing to think about was a board of directors. I would need someone from the community, someone who understood the nonprofit landscape, and someone who could make donations. Eventually, we would need a lawyer and an accountant. But for now, the bare minimum would do. My mind immediately went to an old friend from Smith who just happened to work for Atlanta-based CNN as the head of its corporate responsibility arm. She said yes. Then I looked for a community representative, someone who knew and interacted with the kids already. I asked the principal of a local elementary school to serve on the board and she agreed. After that, I approached a customer of the café who lived in a fancy neighborhood. Finally, I put myself on the board and we became a group of four.

While I waited for the response from the IRS to our application, I collaborated with a friend to design the visual components of the organization. Eric was the husband of my friend Padea who worked for the refugee resettlement agency in town. Eric, a graphic designer, came up with many iterations of a Fugees logo, taping each one to a wall so we could stand back and study them. I would pull down the ones I didn't like and circle certain elements of the ones that I did. What emerged over many nights was a logo that from a distance resembles a soccer ball but on closer inspection reveals a group of people, heads and hands joined together: everyone coming together to solve problems, everyone working together to make our communities stronger.

We spent more evenings craned over Eric's Macintosh as we pieced together a website — perfecting the layout, checking links, refining the copy. We made sure the donate button was front and center.

These were exciting days. The air felt like it does before a thunderstorm, charged with possibility. We were going to make a real difference in the lives of these refugee families. After the website went live, I logged in and out of the admin page constantly, checking for the surge in visitor traffic that I just knew was coming. Except it never did. Some days we had three people click on our page, some days zero. A couple of months after I applied for nonprofit status, I received a letter saying that the Fugees Family was now an official 501(c)(3) recognized by the Internal Revenue Service. We had a board and a budget and a website with a big donate button. All of this was met with resounding silence.

While one endeavor was barely beginning, another was crashing and burning. The café was bleeding money. Sales were stagnant. Payroll was a puzzle with too many pieces. The power went out once and I lost a week's worth of inventory that I couldn't afford to replace. For the second time since being granted asylum, I was broke. I had less than five hundred dollars in my checking account.

On the advice of friends, I went to see a lawyer. Because I didn't have the money to pay back my investors, the lawyer advised me to cut my losses. So at age twenty-eight, I filed for bankruptcy. I had never failed so miserably in my life, and I found myself in a familiar place — rock bottom. In some ways, it was similar to being disowned by my parents — I didn't know what was next, wasn't sure how I would make ends meet. But now, on top of losing my family, I had lost the American dream, the hope I had held on to for so long. Immigrants and refugees are promised a land of opportunity where hard work equals success. Failing to make it in America triggered a severe case of survivor's guilt. How many others were desperate for the chance that I had squandered? But the hardest part was failing those who had so strongly believed in me. My self-esteem and ambition were as bankrupt as my finances.

There were about forty of us in bankruptcy court the day of my hearing. An older man presided as trustee, moving through claimants at a no-nonsense pace. When it was my turn, I stood next to my lawyer and answered a half-dozen yes-or-no questions. I was one of a handful of people there for business-related matters; the rest had come because they could no longer pay their medical bills. My own suffering suddenly seemed petty in comparison.

Looking back, I can now see that there was another consolation.

For almost a decade, I had all but abandoned my Middle Eastern identity, and after 9/11, I rarely told anyone that I was Muslim. I didn't hang out with other Arabs, and the only time I spoke Arabic was five minutes a week with the clerk at the international grocery store. In my mind, my country had rejected me. I was like a spurned girlfriend trying to avoid any reminder of the person who had dumped her.

And then I met the Fugees. Hearing their families speak Arabic, watching Nabi rub his mother's feet after a long shift at the hotel the way my brothers and I had done for our mom and grandmother, sitting around a communal meal, or hearing the call to prayer coming from an app on someone's phone — these things reminded me of all the beautiful parts of my culture I had tried to forget. Writing off my entire identity had been a way for me to move forward in a new life in a new country, but now I saw that it didn't have to be so black-and-white. My old and new lives, my Eastern and Western lives, were converging. I felt something that I hadn't felt since I was a young girl snuggled up next to my grandmother on the sofa. I felt at home.

Filing for bankruptcy was one of the most difficult, most embarrassing things I have ever done. I wanted to lock my apartment door, shut the blinds, get in bed, and never get out. But I couldn't. I had people who needed me now. As it turned out, I needed them, too.

When it was time to clean out the café, it was the Fugees who showed up. Not my former employees, not my friends in town, but Habib, Nabi, Aziz, Shaida, Jerome, Biko, and Nathaniel. The Afghan boys volunteered to sell the furniture out front; I found them haggling over the price of tables and chairs with surprised buyers, using the skills they had learned during their rug-selling days in Pakistan. Jerome and his brothers scrubbed the kitchen, and their mother sent along a one-hundred-dollar bill for them to give to me.

"Ma said you can stay with us," Biko told me.

I accepted Betty's money, though I felt as I imagined she had when I'd bought groceries for the family. Grateful but ashamed.

It hadn't been long since I'd sat down with Betty to try to figure out her own budget. I had learned about income inequality at college, I had read *Nickel and Dimed* and *Savage Inequalities,* but until I went over and over those numbers with Betty, I had no idea how impossible it was to live on minimum wage. One bill stood out to me, the one from the International Organization for Migration.

"What is this?"

"This is for plane tickets."

I was stunned to learn that the IOM doesn't cover the cost of transportation to the United States. Instead, it provides refugees with an interest-free travel loan; Betty had to sign a promissory note to repay it before getting on the plane. As soon as she landed, Betty was $10,000 in debt. What could be more American than that?

The family's story came out in bits and pieces over the dinner table or during rides home from practice. Betty and the boys had survived two Liberian civil wars, some of the most brutal conflicts in modern history. Liberian dictator Charles Taylor was the first leader since the Nazis to be convicted of crimes against humanity by the World Court for his forces' widespread use of torture, rape, sex slavery, human sacrifice, and child soldiers. The family had personally endured one form or another of Taylor's atrocities, and like 1.2 million other Liberians, they had become refugees. Of all my players, the Liberian kids were the hardest to reach. Betty helped me to understand what they had been through but also tried to warn me that some kids were too far gone. "Find the good ones," she would say.

I spent lots of nights after practice with Betty and the boys, getting acquainted with West African cuisine. Betty worked miracles in her cramped and aging kitchen, serving up fried fish and *fufu,* as well as cassava-leaf soup, a thick green stew served over rice. I knew the dish was notoriously spicy, and the family all watched closely as I took my first bite. In seconds, tears rolled down my face. An angry heat blossomed in my sinuses.

The boys began to giggle.

"Ma! I told you she can't eat spicy!" Jerome scolded.

"I only put in three!" Betty protested. Apparently, Betty usually made cassava-leaf soup with seven habanero peppers. Perhaps the prayer rug she later sent to practice with Biko — a gift for me for Eid al Fitr — was her way of making it up to me. It wasn't the first time a member of this Christian family had respectfully acknowledged my faith.

Because the family didn't have a car, I often took one of the boys to the grocery store when I did my own shopping. It was also a good excuse to keep them away from the bad influence and the frequent violence of their apartment complex. One day, Jerome and I stood side by side and looked over a display of breakfast meats. I felt his eyes on me as I reached for the turkey bacon.

"Why do you get that kind?" he asked.

"Muslims don't eat pork," I said. "Pigs are dirty, and they eat their own poop."

Jerome wrinkled his nose. "Do you eat chicken?"

"We do."

"Fish?"

"Yes."

He was silent for a moment, then said, "Okay, I am a Muslim, too, then."

I stifled a laugh. "I think you should talk to your mom about that."

"No, I'm going to be a Muslim like you," he said with the utmost confidence. When I chose turkey sausage, he also chose turkey sausage.

Moments later, we pushed our carts down the frozen-food aisle.

"Can I get a pizza?" he asked. He pronounced it *pisa*.

"Sure, pick out a pizza."

Jerome opened a freezer door and grabbed a pepperoni pizza.

"Oh, Muslims don't eat pepperoni," I said.

"You don't eat no pepperoni?"

I shook my head. "No, it's pig."

A pensive look came over Jerome's face. "Coach?" he said. "I ain't Muslim no more."

I had heard lots of objections to Islam, but pepperoni pizza abstinence was a new one.

When Jerome asked me to come to his elementary school graduation, I knew his request was just as much about getting his mother there in my car as it was about my attending. I was happy to do both, but it took a little convincing to get Betty onboard. She said she didn't know anyone at the school, and I could tell that she felt uncomfortable about the idea.

"This is a big deal," I told her. "You want to see him walk across the stage. And we're going to get ice cream after!"

When the night arrived, I sat next to Betty in the crowded auditorium watching kids accept their diplomas and hug their teachers. When it was Jerome's turn, Betty and I beamed at each other with proud smiles. Betty looked celebratory in a vibrant African dress, and her posture changed then, as if she had grown a few inches taller after seeing her son cross that stage.

At the end of the ceremony, the principal thanked everyone for coming then quickly added, "Will the following kids please stick around." Jerome's name was on the list he read aloud. The house lights came on, and as most of the crowd emptied out of the gym, the remaining parents exchanged knowing looks and grimaces. I didn't know what was going on, but I could sense that it wasn't good.

"These students will not be moving on to the fifth grade," the principal said. "Parents, please talk to your child's teacher for next steps."

When Jerome found us in our seats, I asked him to show me who his teacher was. He pointed toward a woman who looked to be in her forties, talking earnestly with a set of concerned-looking parents. I nodded to Betty and the three of us walked over.

"Can you tell us what's going on?" I asked, when it was our turn.

The teacher looked at Betty then at me. Perhaps because I spoke first, she assumed that I was a translator.

"Will you explain to her that her son is not ready to go to fifth grade."

"You can tell her — she's right here."

"But she doesn't speak English."

Betty suddenly spoke. "He came to school every day. I made sure."

"Yes, he did, but he didn't pass his CRCT."

I kept my hands on Jerome's shoulders, which felt tangled up with dread.

"Coach?" He turned to me. "Does that mean I have to stay here another year?"

"You're not staying here another year."

I couldn't explain to Betty what had happened. I didn't understand it myself. Why had they let him walk across the stage if he hadn't passed? Why didn't anyone tell Betty prior to that night that her son was failing? Why didn't a single person in the school even know Betty's name?

In the car on the way home, Betty was angry with Jerome. "How did you fail?"

"It's not his fault," I said.

"He's the only one left," she said. She meant that of her three sons only Jerome still had promise. The older two had seen too much savagery, endured too much pain. For them, success had been simply staying alive.

A profound sadness threatened to swallow me up. I kept glancing in the rearview mirror at Jerome, who stared silently out the window.

"Ready for ice cream?" I asked.

Jerome returned my glance with a weak smile and a nod.

It was dark outside when we collapsed into the corner booth at McDonald's. The last thing I wanted was ice cream, but I ordered cones for Jerome and me. While we ate, I asked him silly questions and tried to make him laugh. Betty was quiet, a million miles away. Even her dress seemed drained of its color.

I glanced at my reflection in the restaurant window. It wasn't hard to imagine — change a few details of my family's story, and I could have been Jerome. This could have been us.

I had tried to improve as many aspects of my players' lives as I could, but one element kept sabotaging our progress. Their education.

I thought of that day back in 1983 when I was eight years old, just a little younger than Jerome was now, when my grandmother took me to the Palestinian refugee camp. On the drive home, my grandmother was very quiet. I could tell she was lost in her own thoughts.

An hour later, seated at dinner with platters of food in front of us, I announced: "I will give away all my toys and books to the kids in the camp." I looked over at my grandmother.

"How is that going to help?" she asked.

"They will feel good, and they can read and play." This made perfect sense to me.

"It will make *you* feel good. They can't read if they don't go to school, and toys don't fix problems."

"Then I am going to fast until there aren't any more refugees!" I declared.

"You will fast until the day you die, Lamloom," she replied gently. "We need to stop these wars."

A few years later, there was a cancer walk at our school. We all received a sign-up sheet and instructions to recruit sponsors who would pledge money for every kilometer we walked.

No one asked me to explain where the money was going until I took the form to my grandmother.

"Does this money go directly to the people with cancer?" she asked.

"Um, I don't know. They didn't tell us."

"And what next? What will you do after the walk is over?"

My grandmother never let me off easy.

In high school, as part of my bid to join the National Honor Society, I was required to tutor younger students once a week after school. I thought that this would surely make my grandmother proud.

"Every week for the whole semester," I boasted.

"What next? What about after the semester is over?" she asked. "Will they still need to be tutored? Who will tutor them then?"

Over and over, my grandmother taught me that while charity was often a one-and-done thing — secondhand toys, compulsory community service, an evening walk around the park in a souvenir T-shirt — truly helping others required much more than haphazard gestures. *"Shoo baidein?"* my grandmother would always ask me. *What next?* She urged me to consider the needs and feelings of the people I wanted to help, to put myself in their position.

I could no longer stand by and offer piecemeal solutions. No more gestures. I had to commit. *Shoo baidein?* What I would do next was something radical and yet simple: a school that was designed for the children who had been robbed of their childhood so they wouldn't be robbed of an education as well.

PART II

FIFTEEN YEARS
IN FIFTEEN MINUTES

I N THE DAYS LEADING UP TO MY 2017 TED TALK, RUMORS AND horror stories circulated among the speakers like a bad cold.

If you go over your time, the producers will cut your mic, someone said. *If they don't like your outfit, they'll make you change. Remember that famous television producer whose teleprompter got stuck? She just froze up there.* Apparently, that didn't go over well in front of a notoriously tough crowd, some of whom were paying tens of thousands of dollars for a seat in the audience. Those people were hard to impress; *they almost never give anyone a standing ovation.*

It had been twelve years since the evening I had sat in McDonald's with Jerome and Betty, the smell of burnt grease hot in my nose, a grim hopelessness sitting like stones in my stomach. Now I was perched in the green room next to the TED stage at the Vancouver conference center. David Miliband, a former member of British Parliament and president of the International Rescue Committee, was nearing the end of his speech, which meant I was mere moments away from being introduced.

"One, two, three," I said to myself, counting the breaths I pulled deep from my belly, as Gina, my speaking coach, had told me to do. "Come on, get it together." I rubbed my palms on my pants, the brand-new jeans that had been delivered to the hotel that very day. My friend Diana insisted that I ditch my old jeans and buy a nice pair for the occasion. "I promise you, they will make all the difference," she said, when I balked at the price.

I popped another lozenge. Since I had arrived in Vancouver four days ago, cough drops and black coffee were about the only things I could manage to keep down. Coffee cups were scattered around my hotel room, where I had been endlessly rehearsing my talk while studying my delivery and posture in the full-length mirror. Next door, another nervous perfectionist, a cellist named Josh, practiced his performance over and over; hearing the warm notes of Bach's Cello Suite No. 6 through the wall gave me a bit of comfort.

The only time I had left the hotel room during those four days was for sessions with Gina and to take long walks around the city as I listened to a recording of myself on headphones. I'd charge through the mist along the harbor, hands shoved deep in my jacket pockets, making mental notes of where to pause longer, what phrases to emphasize more. Gina had said this would help sear every last word into my memory. Whatever Gina said, I did. I roared like a lion to relax my mouth, I stabbed the air with my tongue to open up my throat, I made my toes into claws to grip the floor beneath me to ameliorate my habit of swaying while speaking. I wouldn't have a copy of my speech to clutch or a podium to hide behind. It would be just me and my fancy jeans alone on the stage in front of world leaders, CEOs, and celebrities, the countdown clock glowing above their heads reading 14:59 in burning red numbers.

Imposter syndrome had kicked in full force the moment I walked into the conference center for my first rehearsal and quite literally bumped into Jeff Bezos. When I looked up at the banner to find my name among the week's speakers, I saw Elon Musk's right under mine. Al Gore was there; so was Steven Spielberg. Serena Williams, who had just won the Australian Open *while pregnant,* was giving a talk. Oh, and the Pope was going to deliver remarks from the Vatican. The Pope.

At my first rehearsal, I flubbed my lines. The speakers before me had all killed their run-throughs, but the photos I had chosen to accompany my talk — now blown up to fit the two-story screens that encircled the stage — kept throwing me off. It was hard to focus with giant images of my students, my grandmother, and a decimated Aleppo hovering behind me.

It reminded me of my performance in the eighth-grade production of *The Owl and the Pussy-Cat.* Until then, I mostly had been part of the backstage crew for school plays, working the lights or the props. But that year, my English teacher recommended me for the role of the turkey, insisting that my recitation skills would translate to the stage. Reading aloud in class, though, is not the same thing as acting, and during dress rehearsal, I tripped over every other word. On the way back to the dressing room, I grabbed a familiar headset to listen in to the backstage chatter.

"Was absolutely terrible," the director was saying. "And now it's too late to replace her." I ripped the headset from my ears.

I had to keep reminding myself that I wasn't that thirteen-year-old girl anymore. That it wasn't about me. It was about the students and the families, about the growing numbers of refugees forsaken by governments around the world, about an escalating antirefugee sentiment that was turning the work I did into a political issue. The election of Donald Trump had emboldened many others to express their long-concealed racism and bigotry. I had always told my players and students to walk away when things got ugly, but that was getting harder to do. It wasn't time for stage fright or shame; it was time to speak up.

The truth was that, as nervous as I felt about tripping or stuttering, what I was most terrified of was missing this opportunity. Sure, no one was going to hand me an oversize check at the end of my speech; confetti wouldn't fall from the rafters. But this kind of exposure, I knew, was priceless. If I could nail this talk, doors would be opened, seats pulled out for us at the table. Despite the antirefugee rhetoric coming from half the country, I truly believed that the vast majority of people were good people; they were just misinformed.

"Tell your stories," I repeated over and over to my students. Our stories have the power to change hearts and minds. It was time to put my money where my mouth was.

Fugees Family had been written about in every major news outlet in America. Our team had inspired dozens of articles, and our school was the subject of countless feel-good segments for morning television shows. But as great as all that attention was, our story was always told through a filter; it always ended up feeling like someone else's story. This was our moment to speak for ourselves without being edited or condensed into sound bites. This was our turn.

But how to fit it all in? I felt as if I had lived a dozen lives in the last thirteen years. The boys I had found in the parking lot that day were scattered around the country, now in their twenties. Some had stayed in touch; others were lost to distance and time. But for every one who left, three more showed up in their place. If my first year with the Fugees was a trial by fire, the fire had only grown brighter and hotter since then. There were, it turns out, more Lewises and Jeromes and Habibs and Amadous than I could fit into a hundred team vans.

We started the school in a Clarkston church basement. There were six boys and one teacher. At first, we called what we were doing a "program," a way to get the kids caught up before we mainstreamed them into public schools. But as six students turned into twelve, twelve into twenty-four, and twenty-four into thirty-six; as we went from single sex to coed; as we hauled all the desks and chairs from the church basement to a three-bedroom house, I began to think that—despite what everyone had told me—a zero-tuition school for refugee kids could work. Not only *could* but *must*.

Hundreds of students later, we had accomplished so much to be proud of. Kids who had arrived illiterate and dismally behind their peers had learned to read and write, and had gone on to college. Kids who had come to us quiet and withdrawn blossomed into confident young people, embracing their new home while being proud of the culture that had shaped them. Of course, we had endured horrible losses: students dropping out, students landing in jail, the deaths of two of my former players. Fundraising was a constant battle; a recent round of layoffs had left me demoralized. It was a roller coaster, this journey, with thrilling highs and devastating lows. And now we were on track to open our second school, this one in Columbus, Ohio, where I would soon move with my wife and children.

Emily and I had married in 2012. Both Smith College graduates, we hadn't really known each other while we were in school, but we met when we returned to Northampton in 2011 for a conference on education. At the time, Emily was working in New York City at a Quaker school for students with learning disabilities. We fell in love and quickly braided our lives — both personal and professional — together. In 2014, Emily gave birth to Leila; in 2015, Zeina arrived.

The stalemate with my family had given way several years before that when my mother, out of the blue, called to invite me to a cousin's graduation in Virginia. Months later, she, my father, and my sister landed at Hartsfield-Jackson in Atlanta, the first time we had all been together in more than a decade. It wasn't an easy or altogether peaceful reunion, and my father had stopped talking to me again when I emailed to say that I was marrying Emily, not just a woman but a Jewish woman. My sister and I remained close, and my mother still called once a week to check in on our growing family.

When I found out I would be giving a TED talk, I called to warn her that I would be "coming out," as it were, on a pretty big stage.

"Why do you need to do that?" she asked. For my mom, my work was always a mixed bag. She was proud that I was doing Allah's work and got a thrill out of the media attention we received. But to her, fundraising (a word that doesn't have an Arabic equivalent) looked a little too much like begging, and she could never understand why I would want to talk about my private life in public, breaking what is perhaps still the Middle East's greatest taboo.

"Mom, everybody already knows," I said. In fact, I had already kissed Emily on TV when I was named a Top 10 CNN Hero the previous December.

"What will everyone think?" She wasn't really asking me; she was just thinking aloud. She knew I didn't care what anyone thought. And for me, it was so important to get up on stage and say all of these things together for the first time.

I am an Arab, I am a Muslim, I am an immigrant, I am gay.

Before we hung up, my mother finally addressed what was actually her most pressing concern: "What are you going to wear?"

I considered telling her about my expensive new jeans but just couldn't help myself. "White Adidas sneakers," I said.

She unleashed a string of Arabic expletives.

As I heard the applause for David Miliband begin, my mind flipped back through the people who believed in me, who saw things in me I couldn't always see. My grandmother, whose example was still my North Star, the only reason any of this was possible in the first place. My middle school English teacher, who never let me turn in inferior work; my high school volleyball coach, who taught me to visualize what I wanted to manifest; Emily, who had instilled in me a radical confidence I hadn't known I was capable of.

"Everyone in that audience has something to learn from you," she told me, and I knew she was right. I deserved to be here. I had earned it.

"Ladies and gentlemen, please welcome to the TED stage soccer coach and refugee activist Luma Mufleh."

I took one more deep breath and put one foot in front of the other. Fifteen minutes later, the audience rose from their seats to give me

— and the story of the Fugees — the longest standing ovation in TED history.

There was never a grand plan. There wasn't a moment when I thought to myself — *This is what I do now; I lead a school for refugees.* I saw kids being deprived of an education, families struggling despite their coveted American addresses, and I did what I could to make their lives better. No school I found was considering the specialized needs of my community. It was easier and more effective just to do it myself.

I had grown up in such a suffocating, restrictive culture. In America, the freedom I had to fix the problem I saw in front of me was an irresistible privilege.

Ending up in education wasn't wholly unexpected for me. During the Gulf War, my high school, run by the American embassy in Amman, was hollowed out by parents eager to get their families away from the encroaching conflict. When our campus was vandalized with messages like SADDAM WILL WIN! and DEATH TO THE ALLIES, the school was closed as the rest of the embassies were evacuated. Everyday life sputtered to a halt.

After a few months without instruction, the small group of students left in Jordan tiptoed back to school, where a skeleton staff was doing all they could to keep the lights on. That meant that everyone — teachers, administrators, and students — had to stretch our time and talents to fill in the gaps. Students wrote the morning announcements. We planned the field trips. Looking back, I think of it as a kind of crash course in the time and effort needed to run a school.

I knew, though, that I would need a lot of outside help with the educational component of Fugees Family. I stayed up late and reread old books from college. Paul Tough's *Whatever It Takes* was the first book I had read about an approach to education that factored in students' families, their neighborhoods, and other outside influences. Jonathan Kozol's *Savage Inequalities* had struck me as exaggerated when I first read it in my early twenties; after all, I thought that Americans complained about everything. (*If they felt life was tough here, they should try living in the Middle East,* I naively thought.) But now I could *see* the disparity Kozol described in the lives of my players.

I found a paper published by the Stanford Graduate School of Education about how long it takes students to attain English proficiency. The authors called the expectation that kids could learn a new language in less than a year "wildly unrealistic." Instead, researchers suggested that it took about four to seven years of total immersion to gain mastery of the language and that, in the meantime, students needed extra support to meet academic milestones while still acquiring English. No wonder my players were floundering.

These texts were validating—and empowering. So I took the next step. Our first classroom in the church basement was rent free, and I found a recent Harvard grad who would teach our first six students. After spending years with the Fugees and earning the trust of their parents, it wasn't difficult to convince them to give my idea a try. I promised Lewis's mother that he would learn to read, and she didn't doubt me. I wasn't *exactly* sure how we would accomplish this, but I knew from coaching him that Lewis, full of heart and determination, was more than capable.

The first year, we worked with six boys in the sixth grade. The second year, we had twelve. The fourth year, the refugee parents of girls approached me to ask if I would accept their daughters into our program, which was gaining quite the reputation. The parents had seen some boys in their communities make complete turnarounds academically and behaviorally. They were impressed by the respectful and polished young men the boys were becoming.

I had never intended to run a boys-only school. Boys are just who showed up to the soccer field. Their sisters had come out to play a couple of times, but none of them could commit to the team; their parents expected them to be home for housework and childcare. I, too, had grown up in a culture that placed a heavy domestic burden on females: I knew how ironclad those roles could be. But now I had the advantage. Our school had impressed these parents as a place where kids worked hard and stayed out of trouble. The kind of place they could send their daughters.

I told them that their girls could attend Fugees Academy if they also played soccer — the team was still an integral part of our program. They tried bartering with me at first, asking if the girls could play volleyball, if they could leave practice a bit early to do chores. I didn't budge. It had to be equal.

We enrolled nearly forty students that year, thirty-two boys and six girls, all of whom entered sixth grade. We now represented grades six through nine with a teacher for each grade.

Those years were scrappy and lean, full of figuring out what worked. From the beginning, we started with the basics — even though our students were technically in middle and high school, we leaned heavily on phonics lessons, filling in the gaps created by their years in war-torn nations and refugee camps.

The time soon came to embark on the formal school accreditation process, which forced us to clearly articulate our mission and firmly establish our methods. There were a few accrediting bodies we could choose to work with, some of which offered simple processes that took only a few months. But when I looked at the websites for all the top schools in the area, I kept seeing the same names — the Southern Association of Independent Schools and the Southern Association of Colleges and Schools. The decision wasn't even up for debate — of course we would go for the gold standard even if a typical bid took two years. Before she came to work for us, Emily had worked on her New York City school's accreditation effort, so she would lead the charge.

A few months before our accreditation visit, I paid a visit to the head of the accreditation team, Bill, a spectacled man with a mop of dark hair. He was the principal of a K–8 school in a northern Atlanta suburb, where annual tuition hovered around twenty thousand dollars — slightly less than what most of our students' parents made in a year. The campus was manicured and charming, and Bill's office was expansive. As he told me what to expect during the three-day site visit, my anxiety ratcheted up.

"You'll want to have a dedicated room for the team, access to a printer, and maybe some refreshments if you can," he said, as my mind played Tetris with the few rooms we had in the church. Maybe if I moved the printer into my office, they could use that. But there was no way three people could fit in my office.

Bill pulled me back to earth with his genuine warmth and reassurance.

"We're so excited to come visit and learn all about your school, your students, and your unique model," he said convincingly.

Unique model was right. This would surely be the first school Bill visited where tuition was covered for every single student (zero-tuition private schools are virtually unheard of), the entire student body qualified for free and reduced lunch, and English was practically no one's first language.

"Just be you," he said.

As if we could be anything else.

On the day Bill's team was to arrive, I used those words with the students and teachers. "Just be you."

Everything in the school was spotless; I had made sure of that. If there were scuffs on the wall, I hung pictures over them. If there were pencil marks on a desk, I scrubbed it clean. The building was run-down and small, the furniture mismatched and donated, our whiteboards not the smart kind. But as I looked around that morning, I thought that it looked good. It looked like *us*.

Things went well. And on the last day of the visit, Bill met with me to go over some of the questions the team had.

"We were a little confused by the admissions process — could you maybe summarize it for me?"

"Well, as you know, we started with soccer. So we have a soccer tryout —"

"Okay, that's what we thought. You can't have an athletic tryout as part of the admissions process."

"It's not athletic."

Bill wrinkled his nose and wrote something down in the notebook he carried everywhere.

"We're not looking for athletes," I said, as Bill scribbled faster. "We bring them out for three days. We look for the kids who show up every day, who give their best, and who tough it out through the hard stuff. Students who don't give up even if they're not the best or the fastest. We also look for the kind kids, the ones who can show compassion — pulling kids up when they fall, passing the ball, a high five here and there."

Bill kept writing.

"We just sit back and observe, really. It's all so subtle. It's funny — we've found that kids who come with huge discipline files are different on the field; they really show their potential when they get to play with others."

"A grit test," Bill said, like he had just figured out a very hard math problem. "You have a grit test!"

"You can call it that. We are looking hard at the character of the kids because we know what they will need to graduate, to overcome the obstacles that have been placed in their way. They have to really want this. But, sure, call it a grit test."

"Great." Bill looked like he was about to finally close his notebook.

"And then we administer an academic test."

"Oh, okay." Bill looked a little more relaxed now; I was speaking his language.

"And we take in the lowest-performing students."

His pen stopped abruptly midsentence as he looked up. "The lowest?"

"The lowest. We want the kids who need this the most. The kid who can't speak a word of English, the kid who doesn't recognize a single letter of the alphabet. Don't get me wrong—even higher achieving refugee students need our school. But we started this school for the ones who need it the most. And we're committed to that."

A few weeks later we heard back—Fugees Academy was officially a SAIS- and SACS-accredited school.

RADICAL INTEGRATION

FROM THE BEGINNING — AND EVEN NOW, FIFTEEN YEARS later — the most common objection to a school for refugees is the notion of segregation. It was a word the director of the charter school used on that sunny day on the sidewalk in Decatur, and it was a word I would hear many, many times again.

I get it. Segregation is a loaded term informed by an ugly history. For nearly a hundred years after the end of slavery, segregation was used to keep Black people poor, unempowered, and disenfranchised. When *Brown v. Board of Education* outlawed segregation in public schools, it was a momentous step forward for African Americans, at least in theory. I remember learning about the landmark decision in my American history class in high school and thinking how revolutionary it was; in my mind, the United States was the pinnacle of equality. The shining city on a hill. Years later, that illusion was quickly shattered by the experiences of my players.

As progressive as *Brown* might have seemed, its intent proved far more ambitious than its implementation. According to recent reporting in the *New York Times*, "More than half of the nation's schoolchildren are in racially concentrated districts, where over 75 percent of students are either white or nonwhite." Our public education system is, by and large, still segregated by race. As if that weren't troubling enough, the *Times* goes on to report that "school districts that predominantly serve students of color received $23 billion less in funding than mostly white school districts in the United States in 2016, despite serving the same number of students." Twenty-three billion dollars.

Nearly seventy years after *Brown v. Board of Education,* our school systems are anything but equal. I witnessed that firsthand in my visits to schools around Atlanta. What I saw in those classrooms was arguably a more insidious form of segregation, one that is evident in skin color, yes, but also in harder-to-see divisions like income and opportunity. In those schools, my players were othered. They were made ashamed of the accents they inherited and the names their mothers had given them. They were told — implicitly and explicitly — that they were less than, that they didn't matter.

I'd like to think that anyone would have been outraged by this. For me, though, it was a bitter reminder. I knew exactly what that kind of exclusion and quiet contempt felt like, how it could seep into your being until it began to sound like your own voice inside your head.

Nestled in his recliner, my grandfather held court over the two rows of couches at his feet, each crowded with uncles and aunts, my father's thirteen siblings. My cousins and I sat on the floor. Everyone — children and adults — was transfixed by the evening news. Jordan's first parliamentary elections after King Hussein had dissolved the lower house a year earlier were being held in 1989, and a woman named Tujan al-Faisal had emerged as a frontrunner, challenging the status quo and upsetting a lot of people in the process.

Everyone had an opinion about al-Faisal, who had been a famous TV anchor, and they were usually strong ones. She was a firebrand, blonde and unveiled. She had recently published an article pushing back against the political ascent of the Muslim Brotherhood because of its archaic treatment of women and practice of sharia law.

To say the Brotherhood wasn't happy was an understatement. It issued a fatwa against her and called her an atheist; no decent Muslim woman would ever utter such blasphemy, it alleged. But al-Faisal was speaking on behalf of the thousands of women in Jordan and across the Middle East who had long felt the same way. She had hit a nerve.

"She should be careful what she says," one of my uncles said to no one in particular.

"They aren't going to let her get away with this," said another.

Aunt Eman spoke up. "She's speaking the truth! This is how we all feel!"

"Oh, come on. In Saudi Arabia, women can't even drive!"

"So we should wait until it's that bad?" Eman asked incredulously.

"She's just a little extreme. She may have a point, but she needs to not say it like *that*."

I heard the debate unfolding around me, but I was lost in my own daydreams. So lost, in fact, that I began to entertain them out loud.

"If she can be the first female member of parliament, then maybe I could be the first female prime minister of Jordan," I said.

The laughter was loud and immediate.

"See what craziness she inspires!"

"*Habibti,* the king appoints the prime minister."

My uncles' laughter wasn't cruel or mocking. They were simply entertained by the fantasies of a child. For a fourteen-year-old girl to dream of becoming the prime minister of Jordan — a country where a grown woman could not leave her home unaccompanied or travel without a male guardian — was as silly as hoping to grow up to be a unicorn.

But, thanks to al-Faisal, these arguments were taking place in living rooms across Jordan. The partisan divide — between the Muslim Brotherhood and reformers like al-Faisal — was putting men who considered themselves moderate in a difficult position. They could choose the Brotherhood, which ruled by violence and fear, or they could choose al-Faisal, who threatened their own status and power.

During the campaign, I watched as my father struggled to straddle that line.

"She's right, Dad; what she's saying is right," I told him on yet another night in front of the news.

"Maybe some of what she's saying is right, but she can't speak like that."

"How should she speak?"

"She shouldn't be as critical and as loud. They will bring her down. I am worried they will kill her."

"Will you vote for her?"

My father never told me whom he voted for, and al-Faisal lost that election. But four years later, in 1993, she won, becoming the first woman elected to the Jordanian Parliament. Her story doesn't have a happy ending. At the end of her term, a government conspiracy prevented al-Faisal from running for reelection, and she was thrown in prison multiple times for speaking out against government corruption and for women's rights in the region.

In the end, my father and uncles were right—al-Faisal was brought down, punished, and forced to flee to Libya.

Maybe her demise would have convinced me to submit to their version of the world if it wasn't for Dolly Parton.

My dad fell in love with Motown and country music when he came to America for college. His vinyl collection from those days—Kenny Rogers, Otis Redding, and Dolly—was his prized possession. We weren't allowed to touch his records but we could listen to them, could be transported through them to other worlds of high-stakes card games and Appalachian love triangles. Other cultural artifacts from the West made their way into our home via my dad's business trips: Maltesers, Nikes, Archie comics, and Betamax. One of those movies was *9 to 5*.

The film's depiction of three long-suffering women who exact revenge on their sexist boss and establish progressive policies in their workplace, including equal pay and an on-site daycare, challenged nearly every notion I had about gender norms. 9 to 5 presented me with a brand of femininity that was aggressive, ambitious, and unapologetic. I memorized every line.

Everything about my favorite character, played by Dolly Parton, screamed female — her hair, makeup, physique, and high heels. And yet. In one scene she throws a lasso around her boss, literally and figuratively dominating him. That she was able to do both of these things — be ultrapowerful while being ultrafeminine — astounded me. Dolly didn't sacrifice one part of herself in service to the other: she was Appalachian and Hollywood, hillbilly and glamour, provocative and powerful all at the same time. I wanted to both *be* her and be *with* her.

The lasso scene played in a loop in my head; any time my uncles said something sexist or my brothers were favored simply because they were male, I'd think about Dolly throwing that rope. But as much as I admired her, I didn't know how to do what she did, to create space for the person I was instead of contorting myself to fit into the ready-made mold that my family and culture had provided. Instead, I learned which versions of myself to play up and which parts to censor. I learned to suppress my nagging sense of injustice and excel in only the acceptable ways: as an athlete and student. And I never, ever talked about liking girls.

So when my dad suggested I apply to Smith College (a school he admired for producing Barbara Bush and Nancy Reagan), I recoiled. The whole point of going to America was to escape the patriarchal oppression of the Middle East. To me, a college just for women sounded like more of the same, a place for sidelined second-class citizens. I could not have been more wrong.

At the end of the first week of orientation at Smith, there was a school dance. For most of my life, school dances were a source of anxiety and dread. Fancy dresses and boys were two things I couldn't

care less about. In high school, I spent the majority of dances helping to hand out drinks or set up tables, anything to save me from
hanging out awkwardly in the corner. But the dance at Smith was
a kind of mandatory tradition; the upperclasswomen came to each
house to make sure we knew to be there.

"It's going to be so much fun," they said almost believably. I *did*
love to dance, and I also wanted to hang out with my new friends. I
decided I would go.

When the fifty members of my house gathered in the hallway to
walk to the auditorium together, I was amazed — and comforted —
by the full spectrum of expression apparent in their outfits, from
Doc Martens and leather jackets to full-on makeup and big gauzy
dresses. We could hear the music thumping across the grassy quad.

As it turns out, "so much fun" didn't begin to cover what we found
inside that auditorium. The dance was the closest thing to euphoria
I had ever seen or felt. Women dancing together, women dancing
alone, women lost in the music, their bodies manifestations of sheer
joy. Within minutes I had been pulled into the fray, just one of hundreds of voices who joined Gloria Gaynor in crooning:

At first, I was afraid, I was petrified

Not one woman was hovering in the corner, not a single one was
tending the drink station awkwardly. I watched as a woman climbed
up onto the sill of one of the room's towering windows. Her eyes
were closed and she sang every word as she tore off her shirt and
swung it around her head.

And I grew strong

For the first time in my life, I let loose on the dance floor, carried
away by the pulsating music and the power of sisterhood.

I was surrounded by strong, smart women at Smith. We were no longer the minority — we were the priority, and our professors all subscribed to the radical notion that female voices needed to be amplified. At Smith, there was no one to talk over us, to drown us out, to tell us that our behavior was unbecoming. In this setting, I was free. Free from the restraints of sexism, yes, but also free from having to be an exception, to prove something to anyone. I could just be me, uncensored, unfettered, and unleashed. I didn't have to fit into anyone else's space. I could — like Tujan al-Faisal and Dolly Parton — demand my own.

All of these experiences and examples led me to approach a group of boys playing soccer in a parking lot. They led me to form a soccer team, to enter a world — youth sports — that was still very male dominated.

In one of my first years coaching the Fugees, we played in a soccer tournament forty-five minutes east of Atlanta. When we filed off the bus, it was like one of those scenes in a movie when the record screeches and all eyes turn to an embarrassed main character. Around us, a sea of white people stopped to stare.

I hoped that I was the only one who sensed it, but Sulayman said, "Why are they looking at us, Coach?"

"Maybe because we just pulled up in our Technicolor bus — everyone else here has an SUV."

"I don't think that's it, Coach," he said.

I struggled to find another reason; it didn't feel like the right time to try to explain racism in America to a twelve-year-old. "Probably because your coach is a woman," I said.

"Maybe that's it. But what if they knew the truth?"

I squinted through the silver lenses of my sunglasses. "The truth?"

"Yeah, Coach. That you are an Arab and a Muslim, too!"

"God help us if they knew that," I joked, but the discomfort in Sulayman's voice felt very serious.

In the early days, I felt that tension and I often tried to ease it. I offered to read our roster aloud for the refs. But after a while, I stopped doing that. It wasn't on us to make other people comfortable. If they struggled through the pronunciations, all the better. Struggling is a part of the learning process.

"How many Mohammeds do you have?" one ref asked.

"It's a common name," I told him.

"Like John?"

"No, like Jesus," I deadpanned.

It was a slow progression, but I started to get the hang of it. I wanted the Fugees to see someone unapologetic about being different. I wanted our school just for refugees to be a place where their identities were, paradoxically, the defining element and therefore irrelevant.

Of course, I was not the first person to think of this. Women's colleges like Smith were founded to give females access to a world outside the domestic sphere despite the persistent assumption that doing so would corrupt young women, society, or both. According to the United Negro College Fund, the nation's historically Black colleges and universities "make up just 3% of America's colleges and universities, yet they produce almost 20% of all African American graduates and 25% of African American graduates in the STEM fields."

But providing underserved populations with a stellar education, as women's colleges and HBCUs have done and continue to do, is only one life-changing aspect of these institutions. The other benefit, while harder to quantify, is psychic liberation or, put simply, more time to learn and less time having to advocate for the basic assumption of your worth. As Toni Morrison said, "The very serious function of racism is distraction. It keeps you from doing your work. It keeps you explaining, over and over again, your reason for being." Instead of fighting for equal treatment, attention, and opportunities, HBCU graduates like Vice President Kamala Harris, Stacey Abrams, Oprah Winfrey, and the singularly brilliant Ms. Morrison could get to work instead.

For students like the Fugees, getting to work meant catching up with their peers — mastering English and making up for lost schooling — and it also means learning a radical kind of self-acceptance.

As a gay Muslim Arab American and refugee myself, it's easy for me to see the internal struggle of refugee children. I know that pull. Between countries. Between cultures. Between identities. Between the multiple versions of ourselves that are created when we are forced to leave our homes. Mohammed becomes Mo. Joyeuse becomes Joyce. Parents who hold on to old languages and traditions become embarrassments, aspects of ourselves to keep hidden. When we are taught over and over again that certain parts of us are less than or not as capable, we try to hide those parts or only show them in certain circumstances. We code-switch. We pass. We look fine on the outside but inside we wither.

Even worse, we internalize the narratives we hear (in school, on TV, from the White House) about refugees. Refugees are the bedraggled masses washed up on the shores of the Mediterranean. They are dirty children in camps with flies on their faces.

Thamein was born in Umpiem Mai, a refugee camp in Thailand, where his family spent ten interminable years waiting for resettlement and selling smuggled alcohol and scavenged recyclables to get by.

When I met Thamein, he was a quiet, soft-spoken, and surprisingly mischievous sixth grader. During the four years he had spent in school in America, he had been relentlessly bullied by his classmates for being Asian, for being Buddhist, and for being short.

On the way to a soccer game once, Thamein spoke up from the back seat.

"Coach, you're an immigrant, not a refugee, right?"

"Why would you think that?" I asked, glancing at him in the rearview mirror.

"Because you are successful. You have a beautiful house, an American family, and a school. You were on CNN!"

For Thamein—and for most of his teammates—being a refugee was synonymous with being a loser or a reject.

Shame is a hard thing to shake. For those of us who have been made to feel that a part of us is abhorrent or undesirable, that shame can linger for years even when we are "successful," even when we think we have freed ourselves from the weight of other people's perceptions. Internalized racism, sexism, or bigotry has a way of burrowing deep into your bones and sabotaging all of your rational attempts at self-love.

This was something I tried to meet head-on with the Fugees—until the day they recognized it in me. Identity—being proud of who you are, every single part—is one of the most important tenets of integration.

The text came from Katie, our after-school coordinator, after I had gone home for the day.

"Heads up. Some of the kids have seen the pictures of your wedding."

The photos—of Emily and me in white, the cliffs and cacti of Palm Springs behind us—were posted on Facebook by a staff member who had been in attendance.

There were two reasons why I hadn't come out to my players and students. The first and most obvious reason was that it didn't seem relevant. I thought that what I did for work had nothing to do with the person I was dating. The second and perhaps real reason was that I was deeply scarred by coming out to my family when I was twenty-one. It wasn't an experience I was interested in living through twice.

It's not that I tried to hide my relationship with Emily from them. The first time Emily came to visit me in Atlanta, there was a student sleeping in my guest bedroom. He was recovering from surgery and couldn't climb the stairs to his family's apartment, so his parents had asked if he could stay with me. Months later, when Emily moved to Georgia, she was immediately a part of the Fugees community, not just at supper clubs and soccer games but actively guiding our accreditation bid and tutoring kids on the weekends. Since I was a coach and then a principal, it would have been inappropriate for me to be overtly affectionate with my significant other in front of my students, but surely they noticed how I opened the car door for Emily or how she just happened to always be over when they came for dinner. *They had to know,* I thought.

"Maybe they do. But they need to hear it from you," Emily said that night when I showed her Katie's text. "How would your childhood have been different if there was an adult in it like you?"

After a night of fitful sleep, I arrived at school feeling anxious and unsettled. It didn't take long to notice that three of my oldest players — Daniel, Samuel, and Lewis — were upset with me. The boys, who now worked for us as coaches and tutors, wouldn't make eye contact when we passed in the hall, wouldn't utter a simple hello. At the end of the day, I saw them in a huddle by the front door.

"Okay, come with me," I said, and shepherded them into my office. The three boys took a seat, arms crossed and eyes on the floor.

"What's the matter?" I asked.

"Nothing," said Lewis. They weren't going to make this easy.

"Look, I didn't tell you — but I didn't lie to you."

This won me no favor. I exhaled and put my elbows on the desk in front of me. I had known these boys since they were eleven. If there had been a right moment to tell them I was gay before this one, I hadn't found it.

"When I came out to my family, they were upset. They didn't want anything to do with me." I felt three pairs of eyes look up at me. "I guess I was scared that this might happen again, with you guys."

"We're not your family," Lewis said. "We would never do that to you."

"I'm really mad you didn't invite us," Daniel said.

"I'm sorry." The boys nodded and I felt the muscles in my shoulders relax for the first time in hours. "So are we good?"

"Oh, no," Daniel said. "You gotta tell everyone. They saw the pictures, too."

I knew they were giving me a taste of my own medicine. At Fugees Academy, we practice community accountability. The good, the bad, and the ugly. Not only do you stand up in front of the whole school to celebrate your successes, you also share your struggles, slipups, and redos.

Of course I needed to tell everyone. They needed to hear it. Just like Thamein needed to hear that I was a refugee like him. The kids needed to be able to see that you can be many things at once — Arab and American, Muslim and gay, a refugee and a success — even if the rest of the world is telling you that you can't. Not only that, you can be brazenly proud of each disparate part of yourself.

By not saying out loud what I was, by not wearing the various badges of my identity with pride, I was turning my gayness into a secret, a story told *about* me, not *by* me. I was also depriving whomever might need to see it as an example. Like I needed to see women like Tujan al-Faisal and Dolly Parton.

It was a cold January day, and bright winter light streamed into the fellowship hall where we assembled as a school every day for morning announcements.

I stood at the front of the room, like I usually did, and Daniel, Samuel, and Lewis formed a loose semicircle around me.

"Okay, everyone, I have something to tell you," I began. I gripped my water bottle with both hands and cleared my throat. "My family comes from the same faith and the same part of the world as many of you do. And I was afraid that if I told you I was gay you might treat me like my family did."

Some of the faces in front of me broke out into smiles, others into blushes. Some kids looked at the floor, probably hoping that this conversation would end soon.

"I'm sorry. I should have told you that I was marrying Miss Emily."

The room was quiet for approximately half of a second before someone blurted out: "Can we have a wedding for you here?"

And then someone else said, "We want to have a party for you!"

Even though I declined their offer to throw another party, I was proud of the Fugees. They had learned that when someone you love embraces exactly who they are it's always cause for celebration. And that when you have a wedding party *everyone* gets invited.

For some of us, embracing who we are is an act of rebellion we have to practice over and over. For many people, starting a school just for refugees is an egregious act of rebellion, an endeavor that calls to mind that shameful word: "segregation."

It's funny to me that these same worries don't apply to Catholic students who attend Catholic schools. No one seems concerned that the children of the rich are barricaded in posh New England boarding schools. The allegations that a school for refugees doesn't prepare them for the real world are laughable; what prepares a child for the real world more than defiant self-confidence? What we have always known is that to successfully integrate a person must know who they are and be proud of it. Otherwise you are merely a caricature, a person playing a part.

At the Fugees Academy, we redefine integration. After all, what could be *more* integrated than a school with no statistical majority, with more than twenty-six countries represented, with dozens of religions and cultures all coming together under one roof? What could be more American than all those accents joining together to recite the Pledge of Allegiance, to sing the national anthem?

When they become a Fugee, our students learn to celebrate who they are. At the same time, they are given the opportunity to try on new hats, to see themselves in new ways, to grow and change. They all become soccer players. Not because I think any of them will go on to play professionally but because movement, connection, and teamwork are paramount to what we do in our school. Everyone also has to play an instrument before they graduate, be a part of a school production, and sing in the choir. Music and performance allow our students to imagine themselves in different worlds, and these activities light up different parts of their brains.

In academics, we meet each kid where he or she is at, not where their age dictates they should be, and we place students in classrooms based on their skill level. We consider their cultures as we explore their learning style and train our teachers to view our students and their families as collaborators. We support parents, inviting them to be an integral part of the school's community.

With newfound confidence, Fugees practice folding themselves into a larger community. Everyone goes on field trips, everyone wears the same red-and-yellow-striped tie, everyone eats the same lunch. Our school day is long, though you won't hear the kids complain about it. They like getting their homework done after school with classmates, tutors, and teachers nearby before they lace up their cleats and burn off the day's stress with their friends. When they get home in time for dinner with their families, they are able to rest and be present, books closed until the following morning.

In short, we manipulate every possible detail to provide a space where students are seen and safe, where they can be themselves so they can and do succeed.

YOU CAN DO BETTER

I N 2016, WE CAUGHT THE ATTENTION OF A FOUNDATION THAT supports the launch and scaling of private schools for under-served communities. When I received a phone call with the news that a team from the foundation would like to schedule a two-day visit with the intention of exploring whether our model could be expanded beyond our single school, I agreed but was skeptical. A number of people had encouraged us to grow, but so far, no one had offered to help us facilitate that growth. It was hard enough to keep one school running.

From the beginning, fundraising felt like an eternal endeavor. To support an enrollment of ninety students, our annual philanthropic lift was 1.1 million dollars. In Georgia, public schools got per-pupil funding, charter schools received two-thirds of that amount per student, private schools relied on tuition and endowments — then there was us. The black sheep, the square peg. Raising the money to do the work we did took up most of my days and kept me up on many nights.

So, yes, I laughed off the idea of starting a second school. It's not that I didn't want to. By the time this foundation called, my day-dreams — when I had time to have them — included a nationwide version of our model. But for us, replication would be even trickier than it is for many institutions. We couldn't simply open up another Fugees Academy an hour down the road in, say, Athens, and spread out from there. We serve refugees and would need to go where the need was — and that meant into other states and other regions.

Before coming to the school, the foundation requested a library of data, test scores, financials, and curricula. During the visit, representatives of the foundation moved through the school like specters, sitting in the back of the room, listening, almost never speaking. They leaned into doorways between periods to watch the kids interact. Afterward, when we sat down to go over their findings, I was gratified to hear that they had noticed the small things about our school: the sense of community, the high standards of our teachers, how our students look out for one another. They wanted to fund a viability study for us to explore growth in places where we could get sustainable funding, states with tax credits or state-funded scholarships (vouchers) for kids from low-income families. A little dumbfounded, I agreed.

It took us about six months of research to settle on Ohio. We found out that Ohio was a great example of how states should welcome and resettle refugees. With strong initiatives in refugee job training and impressive support for immigrant-owned businesses, it's no surprise that Ohio has been successful in helping refugees make the state their home. In fact, aside from Texas and Washington, Ohio resettled more refugees than any other state in 2018. The thought of putting our innovation and replication to the test in America's heartland was appealing.

There were two cities with large refugee populations, Columbus and Cleveland, and Ohio's EdChoice scholarship provided $4,600 per student per year. The Midwest would be a new space to move the needle, a chance to make waves and change minds in a different part of the country. All of a sudden replication wasn't just possible, it was happening.

But there was one more hurdle to jump: we would need a new *me*. For more than ten years with the Fugees, I had been master of all trades: principal, primary fundraiser, and head coach. We couldn't just cut the ribbon on a new building in Columbus and call it a Fugees Academy. We would need a leader and a strong infrastructure — in both schools — a team in place to ensure our students' needs were met in Ohio and in Georgia.

After much discussion with Emily, I knew I would have to move to Ohio along with our family to make sure the new school worked from the start, and we set out to find my replacement in Atlanta. We posted the job ad nationally and the board screened applications. Most applicants were assistant heads of schools looking to move up. Mostly men, mostly white. The board showed enthusiasm about a few of them, but I was reluctant.

The model at Fugees Academy is unprecedented. The population we work with has been neglected and overlooked for decades. Many people nod when they hear our sixth graders perform at a pre-K level but are shocked to see what that truly means. All our students are refugees and have endured trauma. Even the most talented, dynamic administrator would lack the experience or expertise necessary to lead our school.

Because our culture is unique, it is also delicate. It requires 100 percent buy-in. I worried that even the top candidates didn't understand our philosophy, didn't understand our families, and certainly didn't understand refugee identity. Soccer was integral to our school, not as extracurricular but as core. You might not be surprised to learn that there aren't a lot of principals moonlighting as soccer coaches out there.

Was I being too critical? I wondered. *Was I just not willing to let go?*

I got out a piece of paper and started a list: everything I did that was essential to the day-to-day operation of the school. Scheduling, phone calls with parents, disciplinary meetings, working on grant applications, observing teachers, overseeing practice, recruiting students. I quickly blew through one sheet of paper and started another. It was always kind of a joke that I had more than one job, but I could see now how true it was. On one hand, we needed a principal who understood the importance of community in our school and who believed in our academic model. On the other, we needed a coach who understood our families and their experiences, who could get to know the students on a deeper level, and who could provide inspiration and encourage commitment to our school community.

It seemed nearly impossible that we would find someone on the outside who could understand all this right off the bat, so I turned my attention to folks closer to home. Thinking back through the Fugees Family history, two names jumped out at me.

Bev was a Teach for America alum. TFA hadn't been a great fit for Bev, who felt dwarfed and silenced by colleagues who had gone to "fancier" schools than CUNY, where she had completed her undergraduate degree. But she did feel a connection to the students she taught in a Miami middle school, many of whom lacked a stable home life. Bev, like many of her students, had grown up with parents who were either checked out or absent. Despite that, Bev became the first in her family to graduate from high school. Then she became the first in her family to graduate from college, working full-time to pay her way. After TFA, she joined Fugees Academy as a math teacher.

After five years with us, Bev knew the ins and outs of the Fugees; she had helped refine our curriculum and had run our after-school program while getting her master's in counseling.

Bev's only "shortcoming" was that she couldn't navigate relationships with the families the way I could because she wasn't a refugee herself. She also knew nothing about soccer. In fact, the one time we invited her to join practice, she quit after a few minutes, telling us that it was too hard and that we were all crazy. But she watched from the sidelines, admiring the effort and dedication she saw. She understood how vital the team was, how belonging to a team motivated our students and provided another avenue for connection.

I knew I could probably sell the board on Bev.

Raphael, though, I wasn't so sure about.

Raphael was a Fugee. His family had fled the war in the Congo when he was seven. They spent ten years in a refugee camp in Tanzania, where his father died because of a lack of medical care. When Raphael, his mom, and his seven siblings were resettled in America, he could hardly speak English and his future looked bleak.

Raphael was too old for Fugees Academy when he arrived, but he played on our soccer team for three years before leaving to join Job Corps and earn his high school diploma. He dropped out of community college with twenty-two credits, choosing to work so he could put his two sisters through college. He served as an interpreter, made wind blades for turbines, and tutored autistic children, juggling two or three jobs at a time and doing whatever it took to provide for his family.

In Raphael, I saw a coach, but more important, I saw a cultural broker: a young man who understood what our families had been through because he had been through it, too. Students and parents would trust Raphael implicitly.

I spent a few days entertaining the idea and finally broached it with Emily as we cleaned up the kitchen one night after the girls' bedtime. "What about Raphael?"

Emily looked a little caught off guard. She had met Raphael and heard me speak of him often. "Say more," she said.

"We keep looking everywhere for the perfect fit, but the perfect fit is one of us. Someone who truly understands the value of what we've done because they've experienced it. We need a Fugee."

Emily put on her devil's advocate face. "Okay, but he hasn't graduated college; he's never worked in a school. Unless you're counting his internship with us last summer?"

"But he gets soccer. He gets hard work. Families won't have to explain themselves to him. *And* he speaks Swahili."

"Keep going."

"You were right, everyone was right, this is more than one position. If it's Bev and Raphael, the two of them will have each other to lean on. They'll be coleaders. They'll be a power team."

"Okay," Emily said, convinced. "But isn't he in Iowa?"

"Yes, and you know he'll have to clear it with his mom." We smiled at each other, both of us thinking about how utterly devoted Raphael is to his mother, doing nothing without her blessing.

When I pitched my idea to the board, I admitted that it looked unconventional and a little risky (at least on paper). But the more I explained my reasoning, the more I won them over.

With Raphael, the students would be able to see themselves reflected in leadership. They wouldn't have to take our word that refugees were capable and worthy; they would see it right in front of them. While Bev wasn't a refugee herself, her values perfectly aligned with our mission. Community, accountability, safety: these were elements of our culture that Bev believed in.

If I had any doubt about the coleader model, it was dispelled by the students' reactions when I made the announcement. For weeks, a cloud of worry had hung over the building. It was obvious that the students were anxious about who would be in charge when I left and how things might change.

"As you know, we've been interviewing school leaders over the past few months—some of you have been helping with this." I looked out over the tired and nervous faces of morning assembly. "But during the process, we couldn't find the right person for Georgia."

"So you're staying!" someone shouted.

"No. We found the right person right here. Ms. Bev will be leading the school next year. She will be our principal." I saw some smiles break out; each student looked at their neighbor with big eyes and little whispers.

Finally, a brave soul shouted from the back of the room. "Is she going to coach us?"

"Oh, no, I would never do that to you," I said, giving Bev a sly smile. "We are actually hiring another principal who will be coleading the school with Ms. Bev. Next week you will meet Coach Raphael. Raphael is from the Congo. He was a Fugee; he's been a coach for us and a part of our summer camps."

Now the grins were enormous; spines lengthened in pride. And then the serious questions began.

"Is he a good player?"

"Who's his favorite team?"

Being replaced never felt so good.

Shared identity and shared values: that's how we built a power team in Atlanta, and in Columbus. It feels by now like a straightforward philosophy, but it took us years to hone it.

A little more than a year before the school replication study, I met Belinda, the director of the philanthropic wing of a large southern corporation. It was midmorning, stunningly bright, when I walked Belinda to her car. I had done these site visits for funders a hundred times—I felt pretty good about this one. Belinda had toured the school, sat in on a class, spent time with the students, the teachers, and me. In my office, we had chatted about the Fugees Academy's mission and methods, about the foundation Belinda represented, including some of the other schools it supported.

As we approached her car, she turned around to face me. I expected a polite "Thank you," or an "I'll be in touch," but instead, Belinda dropped a bomb.

"The demographics of your staff are . . . interesting."

"What do you mean?"

"They are all white women of a certain age."

It was a statement, not a question.

"Oh, I" — I felt a tangle of defensiveness rise in my chest — "No, we have a part-time music . . ." I tried to meet Belinda's glance, but the sun was behind her, blinding me, as if it were complicit in Belinda's shaming.

Belinda spoke like a disappointed parent. "You're the only one who shares a common identity with the kids. You know how important that is. It can't just be you."

I had gotten pretty good at thinking on my feet during these meetings, but as I cycled through possible responses, I found only predictable excuses. I could say that it was our salary range, that we had a limited pool of applicants. I could say that race and gender don't matter; a good teacher is a good teacher. But I knew the truth and so did Belinda.

I couldn't argue. And not just because I wanted the support of Belinda's organization. I couldn't argue because Belinda was right. It had been nagging me for a long time. At that time, fewer than 10 percent of our staff identified as minorities, and I was the only foreign-born person on the team. It had created an uncomfortable dynamic in which I was the lone intermediary between refugee families and teachers, having to explain the experiences and expectations of one group to the other. Somehow, an "us and them" mentality was creeping into a space that was supposed to be just "us."

I worried that this conflict was bleeding into our day-to-day interactions with students. I worried what message our majority-white staff was sending to these foreign-born students. Had we inadvertently re-created the colonialist infrastructure many of them had seen destroy their own countries?

"I will do better," I said, and nodded.

When I walked back into the building, my staff was waiting.

"How did it go?" they wanted to know. "Do you think it went well?"

"It was fine," I told them, and I closed the office door behind me. I ran my hands through my hair and took a deep breath. I was used to defending our school, but Belinda's comment had shaken me. I remembered another time I had felt this way.

In 1996, when I was a junior at Smith College, I was on the search committee tasked with finding the new dean of the college. There were nine of us — three students, four professors, and two staff members — and together we represented just about every demographic on campus. There was a Black student, a white student, and me, the international student. The professors came from across disciplines, male and female. Our job was to identify three to five finalists culled from the applications that had poured in in response to the job listing Smith had placed in all the major higher education publications and the *New York Times*.

For weeks, I spent hours huddled over résumés and scanning cover letters. Most of the time, I did this with the other two students on the committee, handing the documents back and forth, pointing out notable attributes and achievements. Even at twenty, I understood what an incredible learning opportunity and privilege it was to be part of this process. After we had narrowed our choices down, the president of the college requested a meeting to discuss how things were going.

Ruth Simmons was the first Black president of a Seven Sisters college, and she would go on to become the first Black president of an Ivy League university, leading Brown University for a decade. Simmons's 1995 inauguration brought celebrities like Toni Morrison, Cornel West, and Henry Louis Gates Jr. to the Smith campus. It was the World Cup of academia. There were cameras everywhere, lots of pomp and circumstance.

My memories of that day are utterly clear. Fellow house presidents and I led Simmons's parade through campus. We escorted her onto the stage where she addressed the college for the first time. We wore white and navy and crowns of ivy on our heads.

After the swearing-in ceremony, I raptly watched Simmons's movements around the reception, how she stopped to speak with everyone who wanted some of her time, the confident but approachable way she held herself. I watched as Simmons spoke intently with an older Black woman, placing her hand gently on the woman's shoulder. I didn't recognize the other woman, but whoever she was, I could tell that she was very important, maybe a trustee or an influential donor. I would later learn that the woman was Simmons's high school teacher. Any doubt I may have had about Ruth Simmons was gone after that moment.

As the daughter of sharecroppers and the granddaughter of slaves, Simmons would make access and opportunity touchstones of her tenure at the school. It was those priorities she had in mind when she sat in front of our search committee and told us, "You can do better."

The words sent a charge through the room. As Simmons placed her hands on the mahogany conference table in front of her, I could have sworn she was looking directly at me. Once, in high school, an English teacher had written the same thing on an essay of mine. "You can do better." There was nothing, then or now, more crushing than that.

"Every applicant you sent me is the same. White. Ivy League. You have no diversity here. Will these candidates reflect what we want to see in our student body? Will they best serve our students? You have to read between the lines on someone's résumé. This is an opportunity for you to look at things differently."

The head of the search committee spoke up. "President Simmons, we've had so many applicants and the deadline is so tight—"

"I'll tell you what, I'll have my secretary print out the résumés and white out the names. I think that will be helpful."

I was confused. How would that help?

When Simmons left, the committee was silent for a moment. Then the frustrations began pouring out almost at once. Did she know we were volunteering for this job? Did she not realize the teaching and class loads we were all balancing that semester? After we aired our grievances, a more troubled silence spread around the room. We knew she was right.

So we started again. And with a stack of nameless documents, we began to whittle down a list of finalists. When the names were revealed so we could schedule on-campus interviews, we were surprised to find that our new list had a few of the same candidates on it but a lot of different ones, too. I for one realized that in the first round I had gravitated toward résumés with a woman's name on them. Others on the committee were ashamed to notice that they had been more favorable to American-sounding names. It was an effective lesson on implicit bias.

Before the candidates arrived on campus, President Simmons — now pleased with our selections — encouraged us to ask questions that got to the heart of a person's character, not just their qualifications. The screening portion of the process had ensured that every candidate we would meet had the credentials we were looking for. The interview portion should tell us about the intangibles: attitude, curiosity, humility.

I hosted one of the four finalists, an administrator from a nearby liberal arts school. She was a strong contender with an Ivy League education, but following President Simmons's advice, I noticed things about her I wouldn't have before. How she asked me questions and actually listened when I spoke. How warm she was and how comfortable she made me feel. During her official interview, I liked that she spoke to everyone in the room, unlike other candidates who seemed to make eye contact only with the professors on the committee. Similarly, at our final meeting, President Simmons asked us students directly what we thought of the finalist. And she listened when we told her that this candidate, who would become the future dean of the college, was humble, approachable, and understood the value of a women's college.

That experience has shaped me in so many ways. After the exchange with Belinda, I wondered, *How had I forgotten those lessons?* The more pressing question was—how could I apply them now? What qualities should we be looking for in our staff and how could we recruit the right people?

We needed representation—not just me—that reflected the majority of the students. We needed refugees and immigrants at the top of and all throughout our organizational chart. Nuns lead Catholic schools and women lead women's colleges; it should be a given that we would steer our own ship. The rest of our team should be representative of America, of the world our students would find outside our doors. But those staff members also needed to be closely aligned with our mission and be able to relate to the students' experiences, the grief they had endured, and the grit they had forged. What I wanted was a team of people who shared that common trait —struggle—with the students.

When I looked at my staff, the teachers who stood out were the ones who had experienced great hardship and openly attributed their success to it. The ones who defied the odds and demonstrated to our students what was possible. Mr. Jason, a young Black man who had escaped a chaotic and violent neighborhood because someone saw his potential and sat him in front of a piano. Ms. Ashley, who watched her single mother make sacrifice after sacrifice so Ashley and her sister could go to college. When I asked her in the interview how her former students might describe her, Ashley laughed, and said, "I think they would call me a bitch, but a bitch who loves them." Ms. Ashley is a notorious stickler for grammar, and her expectations for our students are sky-high, but so is her passion.

These were the teachers who consistently held our students to higher standards than the others and didn't accept excuses or mediocre work. They saw struggle and suffering as an asset, not a deficit. They knew what obstacles our students faced because they had surmounted the same ones. They weren't hard on the kids for not understanding something—they were hard on themselves. They weren't there to *save* our students, because they knew our students didn't need saving. They needed an education.

To find more Ms. Ashleys and Mr. Jasons, I had to admit to myself that my hiring philosophies had been misguided. In the past, if a candidate expressed dissatisfaction with their experience teaching in a school, I counted that as a plus. But I hadn't been interrogating the reason for their frustration; all too often (and too late) I would find that their resentment was rooted in interpersonal conflict, not with structural inequality or institutionalized racism as I had thought. Similarly, I had always been drawn to Teach for America and Peace Corps alumni for positions at Fugees Academy. But those candidates were often a bad fit for our school. While this has changed in the years since, the teachers coming out of the programs then were often middle- and upper-class graduates of elite institutions who, instead of being humbled and enlightened by the populations they served, developed the attitudes of benevolent colonizers. I'm sure their intentions were good, but many of them treated the kids as if they were charity cases who didn't need math and reading skills so much as they needed a friend.

I wanted teachers who loved what they did and didn't see their time in the classroom as a stepping-stone into administration. When a candidate told me that their ultimate goal was to be a part of our leadership team, I used to silently cheer on their ambition. But wasn't that just another way of admitting that their passion wasn't in the classroom? That they were simply putting in the time to get a "better" title and higher pay? I wanted teachers whose five-year plan was *to be a better teacher.*

The truth was that the most valuable people in the building were the ones who spent their days with the students. It was why our administrative staff was lean in comparison to that of other schools our size. The way I saw it, the leadership team's primary job was to empower our faculty to perform their best, to control the variables that hindered their performance, and to provide the tools, time, and space it took to get the job done right. This was the same approach I had taken to coaching: control the off-field variables that enhanced or stymied players' on-field performance, things like food, sleep, and even personal problems.

Slowly, I began to push our team to do things differently. Just as President Simmons had done, we began striking the names from the top of résumés. I asked one of our Black staff members to be the first person who screened documents. Immediately, our pool of candidates became more diverse.

We also changed the language in our job postings, asserting that we were a "culturally diverse staff committed to teaching and working in a multicultural environment," and that we "strongly encourage applications from those with a refugee/immigrant background, women, and minorities." Instead of only advertising in traditional spaces — industry websites and corporate job boards — we placed our job ads everywhere, from Craigslist to bulletin boards at community ethnic organizations.

And, like Ruth Simmons had taught me, I began rethinking how I interviewed candidates and looked for questions that would get beyond a list of qualifications and instead reveal someone's character. It wasn't always easy.

THE ART OF
TEACHING FUGEES

"GINA, WHAT IS THIS RÉSUMÉ? THIS GUY HAS SERVED A decade in the military."

"I think the two of you would really hit it off. Just give him a chance?" Gina was my chief operations officer. An African American woman about my age, Gina and I shared tight quarters and an easy rapport.

"Well, I have to — you already scheduled him for tomorrow!"

Gina gave me a mischievous look. A checkmate look. "Just go in with an open mind," she said.

"An open mind? We work with children who have survived war and this person has made a career from war."

The first thing I noticed about William was the contrast between his physical presence (tall and imposing) and his demeanor (humble and soft-spoken). His goatee was graying at its tips, and the deep lines in his forehead made him appear pensive even when he was smiling. My interview with William lasted more than an hour and a half, my longest to date.

I wanted to know about his military experience. He had spent ten years in the marines and ten in the navy.

"I got to see the world," William began. "And out there, I wasn't just a Black man, I was an American." Being recognized in this way for the first time made William feel the weight of that responsibility, he told me. "In some places, they didn't like us, didn't like what we were doing there. It made me realize how people see us and how Americans have an obligation to make the world a better place."

His time in the military also made William hyperaware of the importance of authentic camaraderie, of community at all costs. "When you are on a boat, you are responsible for everyone on that boat getting home safely no matter what. You can't leave anyone behind, and you do whatever it takes to take care of one another."

I nodded. This was a perfect rewording of our philosophy. That everyone in the building was responsible for the successes and failures of everyone in the building. That we would do whatever it took for *all* of our students, not just the easy ones or the high-achieving ones but every single one.

But it was William's experience prior to joining the military that made him such an ideal fit for us.

William struggled mightily with math for most of elementary school. "The teachers would write it on the board and expect us to get it," he said. "I just didn't learn that way."

It was his sixth-grade teacher, Mrs. Brown, who finally made it her mission to help William understand. She told him that she thought he was bored by math, that maybe they could make it interesting. She knew he loved to read mysteries — what was more mysterious than solving for x? Suddenly, math seemed urgent and enthralling. Suddenly, William was *good* at math.

William grew up in Memphis and went to an all-Black elementary school staffed by Black teachers. Everyone lived in the same neighborhood and went to the same church. He remembers a palpable sense of community. Then integration happened.

He was bused to a new school in South Memphis that was full of wealthy white kids. He and his friends from the neighborhood couldn't believe how the other half lived, all the *things* they had, how nice their school was. But it didn't take long for him to realize that even though he was sitting in the same classroom as the white kids now he would not be getting the same treatment. No one wanted him there and that was obvious.

William found a seat in the back of the classroom and kept quiet. He learned that if he didn't make too much noise about what he did or didn't understand his teachers would pass him. Just like Lewis. Just like so many refugee kids I've known. School became dull and burdensome. He wouldn't even think about college for a couple of decades. When he did, he was thirty-five and in need of a plan after his military career. So he got a bachelor's in electrical engineering. He was teaching math, his old Achilles' heel, at a community college when a round of layoffs left him unemployed. Someone suggested that schools were always looking for math teachers, so he applied for a job at a DeKalb County middle school. It had been stressful; he suffered three strokes in eight years. His wife had begged him to retire.

I asked him what he was looking for in a school.

"A place where I can teach. A place where the kids can learn. It sounds simple, but at the county schools, all anyone seems to care about are test scores or passing them through." I gave him a look of tacit agreement. "What happens if a student fails here?" Now he was interviewing me.

"If they fail, they fail, and they need to repeat the grade," I said.

Later William told me that this was what clinched the deal for him. At his middle school, he had been made to pass too many failing athletes, young Black men, like he had been once, floating from grade to grade because no one really cared one way or the other. Social promotion — passing students to the next grade regardless of their skill level — was something William couldn't tolerate.

"And how do you handle discipline in the classroom here?"

"That won't be an issue. If it is, just send them to me."

"You mean we don't discipline the kids?" William looked a little wary.

"Your job is to teach; our job is to make sure the environment is conducive to that. Let the coach handle the discipline." I could've sworn William wanted to hug me.

William checked every box. I liked how open he was about his own struggles and his laserlike focus on the students. Tough love, high expectations, and community mindset — all things his résumé never would have told me.

I saw William to the door, then poked my head into Gina's office, where she looked up at me with an expectant grin.

"You can draw up an offer."

Gina feigned surprise. "So you liked him?"

I knew what Gina wanted to hear: "Yes, you were right."

William turned out to be one of the best teachers I have ever hired. He may not be a refugee, but he shares an identity with our students — as someone who has struggled, who has experienced the sting of exclusion and apathy. Those experiences instilled in him the values our school runs on. And like the Fugees, William is a proud American who has felt the blow of this country's greatest failures and the power of its greatest promises.

The students are the most important people in any school, but the adults in that building will ultimately determine its success. I have made my share of mistakes when it comes to hiring. Every school has paid the price for desperate hires, teachers who are nice people, a good fit on paper, and a disaster in the classroom. So many districts have a rote, inflexible checklist for recruitment: professional development hours, degrees, tenure. But developing a hiring process that is aligned with an individual school's population is so important.

This sounds like common sense, but we have learned to take the time to get to know a candidate. A one-hour interview and a fifteen-minute teaching demonstration shouldn't be all that's required to be handed one of the most essential jobs in our society. We take Ruth Simmons's advice; we dig deep and ask different questions. *Tell me about a time that you have truly struggled. What is the last thing you learned?*

We try to keep the hiring process as localized as possible. The usual suspects — principals and school leaders — should be involved in the hiring process, but so should teachers and students. The more eyes, the more buy-in. The best soccer players I've coached were recruited by my other best players. They knew what to look for and what our team was missing.

It's remarkable to me how often students are not involved in the hiring process. Personally, I have been saved from a number of bad hires by listening to students.

A few years ago, we were interviewing a math teacher. He had made it through the interview process, and things had gone well enough for me to schedule a sample lesson so the students could evaluate the candidate's teaching. I watched from the back of the classroom; everything was going fine, or so I thought. I assumed I would be offering him a job. After he left, I sat down with the students and asked them to share their reactions.

"You can't hire him, Coach," Haben said. "He thinks we're stupid."

I was taken aback. "What do you mean?"

"I wrote down the wrong answer to one of the problems," Haben continued. "And he told me 'good job.' He thinks we are stupid, that we are poor little refugees."

There's no nice way to say it: many, many teachers in American classrooms are trained by academic programs with low to no barriers for admission that adhere to no consistent standard of quality. At the end of their time in these programs, graduates are often thrust into classrooms with little guidance or supervision and are expected to figure it out as they go along. If they're lucky, they'll be promoted to administration by collecting certifications and continuing education hours.

Your doctor spent years in residency; your plumber learned their trade through a five-year apprenticeship. Outside education, professionals are given raises based on performance, not for sitting through a training session or squeaking through another year.

Rewarding mediocrity is a vicious cycle. Too many of our best teachers leave or burn out because they cannot survive in an unfair, unsupportive system. Too many of the teachers who remain are appreciated for their willingness to stick it out, martyrs for the cause. There seems to be an unspoken understanding in the education world that once you're in you're in. When budgets are cut, many schools have a last-one-in, first-one-out policy. No one would run a business like this and expect to make money, so why do we run schools like this and expect stellar results for students? Teachers are as valuable to society as surgeons and lawyers; we should evaluate (and venerate) them in the same way — based on performance.

There are many examples from around the world of how to train and hire teachers to drastically improve student performance. Maybe you've heard about how much recess kids in Finland get or how schools there place less emphasis on standardized tests. What you may not know is that Finnish teachers graduate from training programs that are harder to get into than law or medical schools. They spend years working in "practice schools," public schools affiliated with their universities. They are expected to become not just teachers but experts in teaching.

In Singapore, just because you want to be a teacher doesn't mean you will be one. Every year, the Ministry of Education chooses prospective teachers from the top one-third of graduating high school students. The acceptance rate for Singapore's only teaching institute hovers around 12.5 percent. Teachers-in-training receive a generous stipend while working with a mentor; their tuition is free.

I think we should mimic Finland and Singapore, then take it a step further. We need to reduce the number of degree-granting institutions and put in place a consistent national standard when it comes to teacher training. Tuition at these fewer, more selective schools should be free; students should be supported with stipends and residencies. This kind of reward system would attract the best teachers to the field and allow them the time and security to truly devote themselves to becoming an expert in their fields as well as in their pedagogy. Once teachers are in the classroom, compensation and promotion should be based on performance, not the accumulation of certificates or degrees.

I've seen firsthand the kinds of teachers these superior systems in other countries produce.

Growing up in Ghana, Felicity was surrounded by teachers. Her mother was a teacher and so were her sisters. In this West African country, teaching is a prestigious profession, and admission into a teaching program is highly competitive. Felicity says that getting a degree in education is more rigorous than getting a nursing degree but that it pays off: teachers are compensated quite well in Ghana.

Felicity excelled in math from a young age and was encouraged to pursue it by a professor even though it was considered a "male" discipline. To get her teaching degree, Felicity spent three years learning her content area then one year in national service, where she was paired with a teaching mentor and evaluated weekly on her work in the classroom.

Felicity came to America thinking that she would find a teaching job right away. But her degree was not recognized here. When she applied to a master's program at an Ohio college, some of her credits transferred; she was surprised when the few Bs she earned in Ghana translated to As here. (Even now, Felicity blushes when she talks about those Bs.) She was more surprised when a professor in her program told her that she didn't have to work so hard. She had been so obsessive about her schoolwork that she had barely noticed her classmates' lackadaisical approach. She had figured that attending an American university would be twice as hard as it had been in Ghana.

After she got her degree, Felicity went to work in Ohio for Columbus City Schools as a building sub. It didn't go well. The students defied her; they made fun of her accent. Many evenings she drove home in tears. She remembered that if a teacher in Ghana threatened to call your parents it was time to get on your knees and beg your teacher to have mercy on you. (In Jordan, it was the same.) Here, when Felicity threatened to call home, the kids just shrugged.

Three years went by and there still was no full-time position for Felicity. So she moved on to the city's newcomer center, where she hoped she'd find a better opportunity and be a better fit. Except they said her undergraduate degree wasn't valid there. They placed her among the majority-immigrant support staff, where she worked beneath teachers fresh out of college who had no classroom experience. She says that she has known other Ghanaian immigrants who took work as cooks or janitors because they weren't willing to be instructional aides.

She drove past Fugees Academy occasionally; she had noticed our bright green and yellow bus. She said to herself, *One day I will work there*, and now she does.

Putting Felicity in the classroom was a no-brainer. I didn't need to see her transcript to know that. Between her many years in the classroom, an obvious passion for teaching, and a shared identity with the students, Felicity brings a dynamism that would be easy to miss by looking at her résumé. And the students love her. They tell me that Miss Felicity makes math fun — no small miracle for many of them. And they say that she doesn't give up when they don't understand. She explains over and over in different ways; she says you can do it, keep trying.

I know the students will remember Miss Felicity long after they graduate. But when someone asks them, as we all are asked at some point, about that one special teacher — the one who made learning fun, the one who believed in them, the one who made a difference in their lives — I hope they don't name Felicity. I hope they can't name any one teacher.

I had incredible English teachers who pushed me to be my best just like all my coaches who believed I could do the impossible did. Mr. Peters, who adored Tchaikovsky as much as he did the Beatles; Mr. Marriott, who made me love chemistry; Ms. Carrier, who introduced me to graphic design and computer science. I could keep going.

I hope my students can't name one teacher. I hope they name them all.

THE GOOD OF ALL

A T FIRST, PASCAL HELD HIS REPORT CARD FACING OUT, the way his teachers sometimes read board books to the class. Standing beside him, I gently flipped the paper. "I think it'll be easier if you hold it like this," I said.

Pascal smiled and nodded. Well, technically, Pascal was never not smiling, his twelve-year-old cheeks still padded with baby fat.

"Math . . . 71. English . . . 62," Pascal recited, his halting English inflected with the melodic vowels of his native Swahili. "Music . . . 65. Art . . . 70."

The students burst out in applause. Pascal's smile got bigger somehow and so did his chest. He beamed at his classmates, who clapped and shouted and cheered. I offered my fist and Pascal bumped it.

We typically don't lose our collective cool over Cs and Fs during our end-of-term report-card readings. But for Pascal, these grades represented remarkable progress, and the kids knew it. It had been only six weeks since our last report-card reading when Pascal had held his report card upside down and couldn't read a word of it. I had helped him through it, reading it out loud while tracking with my finger so Pascal could follow. That his scores were in the teens were a surprise to no one.

Pascal had never set foot in a classroom. He had grown up in a small Congolese village without plumbing and electricity, let alone schooling. (The students who recruited Pascal from his new neighborhood, always looking for the positives, reported that he could catch fish with his bare hands.)

To make things more difficult, Pascal had joined our school in October and missed the two-week boot camp we host every September for our new students. During this time, we go over the big-picture stuff: our rules, expectations, and creed. But we also go over things that other schools almost always take for granted with refugee kids —that they know how to dress for school, how to raise their hand, how to hold a pencil. After a few accidents, we realized that we also needed to teach the kids how to ask to use the restroom.

In fact, it was Pascal who showed us that we needed to take our restroom instructions even further. One morning before school, Wendell, our janitor, came rushing into my office, his eyebrows bent with worry.

"What did they do this time?" I asked.

Wendell struggled to find the words. "I just need you to come and see."

When I saw what had disturbed Wendell—that someone had used the urinal like a toilet—I immediately thought of Pascal. "I know exactly who did this," I told Wendell, who must have been very confused by the comment.

I realized in that moment, though, that we had skipped over something essential. Not only with Pascal but with Wendell, too. My job wasn't just to explain native customs to foreign-born students but to explain foreign misunderstandings to native-born employees. If he hadn't talked to me, Wendell might have decided a student was defacing school property. And if Pascal didn't have our guidance, he would continue to make innocent mistakes that hindered acclimation to his new country. For the couple of weeks he had been at Fugees Academy, Pascal had shown us his rough edges. His clothes were wrinkly and unkempt, and his personal hygiene needed some encouragement.

If anyone knew how explicit we needed to be with the kids about things like this, it was me. When I first arrived in America, I didn't know you could flush toilet paper (in the Middle East, our ancient plumbing couldn't handle it). After a few months in college, my roommates had to have a serious talk with me about our bathroom trash can. Emily had once texted from the home of one of our Syrian families — there was no toilet paper, she wrote. She was confused, but she wanted to be sure not to convey anything to the family that could be misconstrued as judgment. I told her to look to the right and she would see a hose.

After the urinal incident, we held a quick assembly with the sixth-grade students about the proper ways to use the bathroom. I shared my own experiences about bathroom customs and confusion to make sure no one felt embarrassed or alone. We also took the opportunity to review good hygiene habits. This didn't feel out of the ordinary; at Fugees Academy, we consider it our job to teach the kids about *everything* that can affect their young lives.

Once we had Pascal onboard with how to use the restroom, we moved on to more pressing matters: getting those grades up. A larger percentage of our students' grades during their first two years is based on developing good habits. Showing hustle. Demonstrating accountability. Part of the reason we read report cards out loud is to show kids like Pascal that they're not alone even if they're failing their classes. And it makes Pascal's success everybody's job — not just Pascal's and his teachers'. Everybody's.

Like so many of my ideas, report-card assemblies began on the sidelines of a soccer game. It was the Fugees' first year and one of our best players, Patrick, had to sit out for failing his classes.

"Why are you on the bench?" I heard one of his teammates ask.

"Showed up late to practice," Patrick lied.

I shot Patrick a look that said, *We'll talk about this later.*

At the end of the next term, I told the boys to bring their report cards to practice and read them out loud instead of turning them in to me.

"When someone on the team has an F and can't play, that affects all of us, doesn't it?" I asked. The boys gave sheepish nods.

"When one person suffers, we all suffer. We have to start taking better care of one another. The way we do on the field. It's not all about soccer and friends. You have to start prioritizing your education. I'm not the only one responsible for that — we all are. If you know your teammate is not going to school, you need to get them there. Even if that means going to their apartment and getting them out of bed yourself."

In the weeks and months that followed, this new transparency encouraged the kids to keep tabs on one another, to make sure morning alarms were set and homework was turned in on time. As much as we want to believe that family and teachers hold ultimate sway over kids' development, peer accountability trumps all. Every child longs for the support and admiration of other children. Making grades a communal effort harnesses that instinct and uses it for good.

Our report-card tradition on the sidelines of the soccer field continued on to school assemblies. Every six weeks, the whole school gathers, grades are distributed, and everyone takes their turn at the front of the room. The few who are failing are asked to stay standing so coaches can get to the bottom of the bad grade. We've found that asking a student, "What's going wrong in math class?" in a private setting elicits a much different response than if we ask in front of their math teacher. When the coach asks the same question in front of a group, the student is less apt to blame a teacher or offer flimsy excuses and more likely to provide an honest assessment of their own performance.

At first, the teachers were uncomfortable with the ritual. In this country, while we love to announce who is earning As, everyone else is supposed to keep quiet about their report cards. (After all, when was the last time you saw a bumper sticker that said, MY KID IS EARNING BS AND CS AT SUCH-AND-SUCH MIDDLE SCHOOL?) But when we make something secret, we also make it shameful. Reciting grades out loud normalizes struggle and encourages an empathetic, cooperative culture. If you're failing, you get to see a team in front of you invested in your improvement. If your report card is full of As, you can see who could benefit from your support. And most important, no one slips by under the radar.

One of our catchphrases at Fugees Academy is "military meets Montessori." When people hear that, I think they imagine some kind of hippie boot camp. But, as William taught me, when we say "military," what we mean is commitment to community. When we say "Montessori," we mean that we meet the kids where they are at — even if they need board books in sixth grade, like Pascal did — and don't move on until they have mastery of the subject. While each child's academic journey is completely individual, they are supported by layers of community.

Every part of our students' day is designed to embed them in additional layers of intentional community. In traditional schools, there are always kids on the periphery, self-isolated or ostracized, who don't have friends or a place to sit at lunch.

I've seen too many schools where community is an afterthought, including my own daughter's. When Leila started kindergarten, her behavior changed significantly. Gone was the effervescent, happy little girl she had always been. She became lethargic and gloomy; she raised her hand at the dinner table. Emily and I hoped that it was just the longer school day or the rigor of the French immersion program she was in. We asked her if anything was bothering her and she said no, but deep down, we knew.

After a couple of issues with the bus (it was never on time and there were fights), I decided to take Leila to school myself. One day, I dropped her off in the cafeteria, gave her a squeeze, and slipped out the door. On the sidewalk outside, something held me back. An instinct. I waited a few minutes, then peeked my head back in. I saw my daughter crumpled on the floor crying. It took all the restraint I had not to walk back in. I waited and watched as student after student walked by, ignoring her. Adults walked by with hardly a glance in her direction. No one stopped, no one bent down to ask if she was okay.

That was my breaking point — not her detachment, not her fatigue. The lack of an empathetic culture, the absence of community. We moved her to a different school the following semester.

At Fugees Academy, this wouldn't happen. Kids can't get pushed to the fringes because there are no fringes. Every child is seen every day.

This starts at the beginning of the day when students are greeted by an adult — a coach or a teacher — and a handshake. I call this "taking the pulse" of the school. As a coach, I could always tell when one of my players was upset or in distress just by the way they walked. This doesn't require superhuman intuition — it's what happens when you pay attention, when you watch and listen day after day. When the adults at the front door of the school walk back to their classrooms or offices, they usually whisper the same names to one another, the students who seemed off that morning, who may need some extra attention.

Along with being seen at the start of each day by attentive adults, students are automatically folded into three layers of support: their class, their team, and their house. Throughout each school day, they move from lesson to lesson with their academic class. After the school day, they have practice with their team. Most kids find their niche in one of these two communities. If for some reason they don't, they can turn to their house.

I didn't come up with houses (and neither did J. K. Rowling). The house system was the invention of British boarding schools, where kids lived in literal houses on campus. But even without the residential component, much of the original intention remains at Fugees Academy—to provide students with social and emotional care traditionally provided at home. In my British elementary school, belonging to a house brought older kids into my orbit, which in turn made me feel special and protected. When it was my turn to be a mentor, I felt empowered and important.

At Fugees Academy, we divide students into four houses, taking extra care to create the right balance of genders and ethnicities in each house. Two captains—one boy and one girl—are elected in each group, which students belong to from the beginning of their time with us until they graduate.

Houses often provide younger kids with a sense of an additional safety net, and they give older students the chance to spread their wings and take on leadership positions that grow their confidence. Older students help with summer boot camp, offering logistical support (how to tie a tie) and moral support (just being there). Following report-card readings, the kids left standing meet with their houses, where someone has always been where they are now and someone else knows the way forward. To ensure that the older students understand their role as protectors (not overlords), teachers, coaches, and administrators constantly model what empathetic leadership looks like.

Houses allow us to ensure that kids are branching out from their own set of friends or from peers who speak their language. We also encourage social engagement and good habits in the form of competition between houses; points are awarded for most books read, most miles walked, best Halloween costumes, and so on. Each week, a different house is in charge of a different chore: taking out the trash or cleaning the tables after lunch. At Fugees Academy, cleaning is never a punishment or debasement but rather an act of service for your school. Our school is our home, our community, and we are all responsible for it.

If the morning handshake is taking the pulse of our school, then these other touch points — class, soccer practice, house meetings — are daily checkups.

Another way we demonstrate to students that they are a part of something larger is by incorporating parental involvement and inviting the whole family to take part in our community.

Most of us have complicated relationships with our parents, but for refugee families, these bonds are often strained by the inverted power dynamic that forced emigration creates. After resettling in America, parents often rely on their children for help with everything from translation to transportation. In many cases, this leads to resentment on the part of the child, who begins to feel that their family is a burden. We actively work to disrupt this phenomenon by assigning homework that allows the parents to be the teacher. Students are required to learn the story of their name, for example, and to present book reports that connect the story to their families' experiences.

And we offer constant reinforcement of the sacrifices students' parents have made for them, taking every opportunity to show them what respect and honor look like.

I am haunted by the ghosts of the mothers I have known. The way Betty resisted an invitation to her own son's graduation because she felt so unwelcome at his school. How Shaida was forced to decipher school forms translated into Arabic because no one bothered to learn that she, like many Afghans, spoke Farsi. The empty seat in the principal's office where Amadou's mother should have been.

I promised myself that our schools would not alienate the people we were there to serve. Gaining a deep and intimate understanding of our community is only the jumping-off point. For example, we know that very few of our parents work a typical 8-to-5 shift. Some work the afternoon shift at the chicken processing plant; some work on overnight cleaning crews; some do both. When we have school events, we stretch them out over an entire day, 8 a.m. to 8 p.m., to make sure everyone can find a window to attend. Other barriers for our parents include transportation and childcare — so we take care of those things, too.

But providing access is the easy part. Facilitating comfort is a bit more nuanced.

Prior to Parents' Day or any event, parents receive a personal invitation via a phone call or an in-person visit when necessary. We remind them that we can't wait to see them and share with them what their children have accomplished. For students with absent guardians, coaches step up as surrogates for the day.

When parents arrive, they are greeted immediately and warmly, and introduced to an interpreter if needed (sometimes these come from the local resettlement agency; sometimes they are older students). Right off the bat, they see people — teachers and school leaders — who look like them. They see the photos of the students that adorn our halls: former graduates who wear sashes embellished with their home country's flag. They are treated to snacks and drinks from around the world, food that is familiar to them.

Everything is designed to convey the tremendous amount of respect we have for them. What I witnessed with my players' mothers were schools that conflated illiteracy with incompetence, that mistook embarrassment for apathy. At Fugees Academy, we recognize the things our parents *have* achieved: protecting their children in war zones, starting over with nothing in a foreign country, working double shifts without complaint.

These small gestures and this overall environment help open up the lines of communication so we can work together toward their child's success. If we can earn a parent's trust, we have a much better chance of winning their involvement, too.

On Parents' Day, our teachers make sure to describe what students have excelled in — not just what they need to work on. We also demonstrate children's growth in ways that are accessible to the parent, who may not have any frame of reference when it comes to academic measures and standards. A few years ago, a Congolese mother reminded us how important this is.

Esther was a single Congolese mom raising five children, including Pierre, a sixth-grade Fugee. Both mother and son were small in stature; both looked older than they were, as if the toll of their experience had been etched into their faces. For Parents' Day, Esther brought along Pierre's siblings, clutching the youngest, a baby, to her chest. We offered to take the baby to the daycare room, but Esther just clung harder, as if the infant was her shield.

She walked slowly through the building, her verdant gown swaying with each step, and she paused to look at the photos. I thought I saw her face soften when she recognized Pierre in one of them. But the rigidness in her jaw returned as she listened to Pierre's English teacher and his math teacher, nodding solemnly as they showed her his grades and a few graphs that illustrated his progress.

Then I escorted her to Pierre's art classroom. I stood in the doorway as she met with Ms. Anita, Pierre's art teacher. Anita dug through the pile of student artwork and pulled out some of Pierre's. For the first time all night, Esther smiled. She radiated. She laughed as tears rolled down her cheeks.

"Pierre?" she said over and over, pointing to the artwork.

Anita nodded and smiled each time. The interpreter stood quietly next to Esther — none of us needed a translation to understand the joy this mother felt at seeing what her son was capable of, the spirit that had survived in him despite the trauma they had endured. The color, the strokes of his markers, told her more about his progress than any graph or grade report could.

Good relationships between parents and schools are not one-sided, however. They don't work when one party has all the power. The connection must be built on equity and reciprocity.

I learned a lot just by being on the field with my players. But even there, I was getting only a fraction of their stories. To fully know them, I had to go to their homes, take off my shoes at the door, and sit around a vinyl tablecloth stretched across the dining-room carpet and spread with dishes of food. It was an accident that I ended up in Shaida's apartment, but the time I spent with the family opened my eyes to the refugee experience, a story I thought I knew since I had also lived it. Over Betty's cassava-leaf soup, I was ashamed to realize that the assumption I had made about her spending habits had been knee-jerk and misguided. And I cannot count the number of harrowing and illuminating stories I have heard over the kitchen sink while standing next to a player as they washed and I dried. There is no shortcut to building a trusting relationship — there is only the time we are willing to spend.

We cannot ask parents to meet us on our turf if we are unwilling to venture into theirs.

That's why at all of our campuses our coaches commit to spending at least one evening each semester with each family. This isn't just a symbolic gesture. It's a free, easy, and effective way to learn more about our students' lives and their families' experiences. Getting to know our families, who often know very few people in their new country, is another aspect of the wraparound instruction we give to our students.

In letting the parents provide food and hospitality, we reset the ballast. They are used to social workers and resettlement agencies treating them as if they were incapable and helpless. So many refugee parents have been stripped of their careers, their usefulness, their dignity. We want them to know that they are integral to our community — as contributors, not passive receivers.

For all the parents like Esther, for all the mothers and fathers who answer when we call and welcome us into their home, there are others who, for one reason or another, are unreachable. Like all schools do, we have students with absent, abusive, or alcoholic parents. We also have parents who struggle to see the value of education — especially for their daughters.

Nour was an Iraqi teenager, sweet and precocious. She wore a hijab on the soccer field and endured the bullying of opposing teams who called her a "Muslim terrorist." Still, she always lined up to shake hands at the end of the game, always impressing me with her perseverance and quiet dignity. After her freshman year, her mother wanted to pull her out of the Fugees Academy so Nour could come home early and help take care of the house, not play sports and attend after-school tutoring. Her mother said that Nour's brother could stay because he was a boy. I spent a few hours with Nour's mom talking to her about the importance of an education and how far her daughter could go. She knew I respected the family's culture but also that I wanted the best for Nour.

Her mother asked, "You really believe that she could go to college?"

I told her that I did and explained the various professional paths her daughter could forge if she was allowed to prioritize her education.

I also told her that if she didn't allow her daughter to stay at Fugees Academy then her son couldn't stay either.

"I knew you were going to say that," she said, and her mother agreed to let Nour continue with us for another year.

Below our students are layers of safety nets, families to fall into when the one at home is dysfunctional or absent or needy or unsupportive. Class, team, house. At the helm of each of them is an adult who knows that student and truly cares about their well-being. A tidal wave of studies has shown that having a caring adult outside the home is paramount to a child's success both academically and emotionally. At Fugees Academy, we have seen the productive and corrective impact of community — when things are going well and when things have gone awry.

We had an incident a number of years ago. Two iPads were missing from a classroom. I was traveling when I got a call from Gina telling me that a small contingent of teachers wanted to search students' bags for the lost computers. Should she let that happen? I told her that under no circumstance would we search bags. We don't treat our students like criminals. Instead, I told her to gather everyone, let them know what had happened, and tell them that if they saw the iPads to please return them to the office.

When I got back, the iPads were still missing. I called another assembly.

"We really need those computers back," I said. "We don't have extra ones." I reminded the students that we are a community, that we take care of one another. We trust one another. I reminded them that my office door was always unlocked and that if anyone took the iPads by mistake they should leave them on my desk.

For two weeks we heard nothing, then one morning an AmeriCorps member came into my office. She said that during a visit to Ameen's house she saw his brothers using the iPads.

I called Ameen into my office. "Is there anything you want to tell me?"

At thirteen years old, Ameen was lanky, with large doe eyes and straight black hair combed to the side. His white button-down billowed around him as he debated his options.

He told me there wasn't.

I let the silence hang over us. I told Ameen to think hard. Minutes went by, and he finally said, "I took the iPads."

In one of the city's other middle schools, this might have been the part where I handed Ameen a three-day suspension. Instead, Ameen and I spent some time talking, thinking about what's right and what's wrong, the harm you cause when you break trust in the community. Ameen is Muslim, so I asked him if he knew what the Quran says should happen to those who steal.

"They'd cut off your hand. Crazy, right?"

"Crazy, Coach."

"Do you think your hand should be cut off?"

"No."

"Of course not. Do you know what would happen if you stole these iPads from Walmart?"

Ameen shook his head.

"You might go to jail. Do you think you should go to jail?"

"No."

"Of course not. So what do you think we should do?"

"I will give them back."

"And then what?"

"Um, then . . . that's it?" Ameen said hopefully.

"Nope. You have to take responsibility and face the consequences. You know what you need to do."

"Coach, no. Please."

"Listen, we won't cut your hand off and you won't go to jail. I've got your back. But your classmates need to know."

We rang the end-of-school bell early to indicate that there would be an all-school meeting. The kids filed in looking confused. We met often, but unplanned assemblies were rare.

Ameen and I stood at the front of the room. I could feel the tension in his body from a foot away. His small hands were balled up into nervous fists.

I put my arm around his shoulder.

"What happened, Ameen?" I asked.

"I put the iPads in my bag after class. I wanted to play on them and I wanted my younger brothers to also play."

"Why didn't you tell us?"

"I didn't want to get in trouble. I didn't want everyone to be angry with me."

"Why was it wrong?"

"Because they are not mine, they are the school's."

"What else do you want to say?"

Ameen turned to the teacher whose classroom he had stolen the iPads from. He told her that he was sorry. He turned back to his classmates seated in front of him. He told them that he was sorry.

I asked the students if they had any questions. It turned out that they had a lot of them.

They wanted to know when, why, and how.

"Are you going to do this again?" someone asked.

"No," Ameen whispered.

"But how do we know you won't steal again?" asked another.

I answered before Ameen could, giving his shoulder a squeeze. "Because he said he wouldn't."

Once the room settled into stillness, I asked all the adults to step out into the hallway. "You know what to do," I told the kids. "You have ten minutes."

I left with Ameen to stand in the hall, where we could hear a few of the suggestions being batted around inside the fellowship hall.

"I think he should run one hundred laps."

Ameen's wide eyes grew wider.

"He should take out the trash every day. I hate taking out the trash!"

"What's that going to teach him?" an older kid asked.

Ten minutes later, Ameen and the adults walked back in.

"Okay, guys, what's the plan?" I asked.

"He's good, Coach," one of the house leaders told me.

"He's good?"

"He took responsibility. He knows it's wrong and he told us he won't do it again. We believe him."

"Great—okay, everyone, get ready for practice and I'll see you on the field."

Ameen stayed frozen at the front of the room, maybe a little shellshocked by all of the attention, by everything that had just transpired. As the students filed out past him, they patted his back. His shoulders began to inch back down and a little smile spread across his face. He was still a Fugee.

Community begets community. Show kids what it looks like to love and trust one another, and not only will they feel supported, they will also know how to support others.

Sometimes the problems with our school systems feel overwhelming and too expensive to fix. One of the best things about cultivating community is that it's free and you can start any time.

It's not complicated to fold kids into webs of community. For us, it's our houses, our soccer team, our custom of kids cleaning up after lunch, and our tradition of having students cook lunch for their classmates on special occasions. But it might look different at another school with a different population. Still, every institution needs mentors and tutors. Morning handshakes don't cost a thing. What counts is that everyone is involved. Everyone gets to feel that they are a part of something bigger, something they play a meaningful role in.

Celebrations are important — and they can extend to cultures and religions, too. We live in one of the most diverse countries on Earth. There's no reason we can't recognize Eid, Holi, and Passover alongside Christmas. In my elementary school, we celebrated Chinese New Year even though there were only a few Chinese students enrolled. In many ways, learning about the custom was more for the non-Chinese students than it was for those who already celebrated the holiday. My life was richer for it.

In an ideal world, we would have smaller neighborhood-based schools that included a greater range of ages. Instead of elementary, middle, and high schools, we could have K–12 schools so kids experience a continual sense of togetherness. But even without a massive overhaul, without an influx of funding and revamped policy, we can begin to create community now.

We are bombarded every day with news stories about how isolated our children have become. How social media has created a culture of self-obsession and fueled vicious new methods of bullying. Schools have the opportunity — and the obligation — to consciously and creatively engender community for refugee children and all children. All we need is the will to do better.

TEACHING CHILDREN
OF TRAUMA

MAJOK WAS FROM SOUTH SUDAN, ONE OF THE BOYS I found in that parking lot twenty miles outside of Atlanta in 2004. He was tall and sinewy, seemingly surrounded by a force field of intensity. Sometimes that energy was productive — during the Fugees' first soccer season, Majok made his mark; he was strong and smart on the field, by far one of the best players. But more often, that energy was destructive, a hurricane churning for landfall.

This volatility reached its breaking point one ordinary afternoon in an end-of-practice scrimmage. The scrimmage was usually the day's highlight for the boys, a little bit of freedom and a chance to implement the skills we were working on. This one was no different; the Fugees were eager and spirited. Ten minutes or so into the scrimmage, Majok characteristically broke for the goal, leaving Elijah struggling to catch up. In a desperate move, Elijah slide tackled Majok from behind, missing the ball but catching Majok's legs. Almost instantaneously, Majok was on top of Elijah, his fists swinging wildly.

Before I could think, I was behind Majok, pulling him away from Elijah. Without missing a beat, Majok let go of Elijah, spun around, and hit me. I must have felt it, but in the moment, the pain didn't matter. I knew that if I didn't control the situation, someone else might get hurt. Instead, I braced my body and found the knobs of Majok's shoulders with my hands.

"Majok, stop it. Look at me."

He hit me again, this time in the ribs.

"Stop it. Look at me."

Finally, Majok's frenzied eyes met mine.

"It's okay," I said, my voice firm but not loud. "It's okay. I got you."

Majok's body went slack. His forehead dropped to my shoulder and the tears began. I felt the other boys begin to move away, knowing that Majok needed some space.

"What are you so mad about?"

"Everything," Majok said, as he dissolved into sobs.

"Okay, just let it go. Let it all go."

I had known before asking that the outburst had nothing to do with a slide tackle. This was early in my days with the Fugees before I learned just how turbulent their lives were, but I had seen Majok's dad around the neighborhood, obviously drunk. His mother was an unsmiling woman never without her brood of young children. Neither of Majok's parents had spoken to me, and I got the distinct impression that this was on purpose. Whatever conflict was now unfolding in Majok's home life no doubt paled in comparison to the chaos the family had fled in South Sudan.

"Come on," I said to Majok. "Run with me."

He didn't ask questions; he just started walking briskly before breaking into a jog. I lasted a couple of laps at his pace, then told him, "I can't keep up with you, but you keep going. Once you feel like your heart isn't hurting anymore, come get me."

Majok ran. And ran. And ran. He ran through the end of the scrimmage. He ran as everyone picked up their bags and scattered in opposite directions, heading for their apartment complexes. He ran as the sun moved behind the trees and the sky turned pink. He ran as I gathered my things and sat to wait for him to be done with running. Finally, he came over to me.

"Coach. I'm sorry."

"In a few years, you'll be taller than I am. You'll be so strong that I won't be able to pull you away."

Majok nodded.

"Your team needs to be able to trust you. I need to be able to trust you. You are a Fugee and Fugees don't act like this. You hurt one of your teammates today and you let the rest of the team down. You know you're a leader — they look up to you."

"I'm a leader?" Majok said, genuinely surprised.

"Yes." I let the new knowledge sink in. "Anger can control you; I know that. I can help you figure out ways to handle that. But you have to do your part. You have to use the tools I teach you, and you need to tell me when you're having a bad day."

"Okay, Coach."

"Sometimes when I'm angry, I count to ten and breathe more deeply." I started counting and breathing deliberately to show him what I meant. "And then, if I'm still angry, I count to ten in Arabic. Still angry, I count to ten in French. And then Japanese."

"You know Japanese?"

"I took karate," I explained. "Running seems to work for you, so if you have a bad day, just come to the field early and start running. Run until your heart doesn't hurt anymore."

A few weeks later, we had a friendly scrimmage scheduled with another neighborhood team. The trash talk before the game continued into the match, but the Fugees were clearly the dominant team, more disciplined, athletic, and cohesive — plus we had Majok. The only way the other team would even have a chance was to neutralize him. There were two ways they could do that: they could injure him or get him tossed out by baiting him into a fight.

They kept clipping at his heels, trying to get under his skin. A couple of times I wondered if I should pull him to the sideline, help him get calm and centered. I hesitated, then it was too late. A dirty tackle took Majok down face-first. He wasn't on the ground long. He sprung to his feet, fists clenched, chest inflated. The Fugees froze; they held their collective breath.

"Majok!" I yelled, edging toward the line in case I needed to run onto the field. He looked over at me, holding my gaze for a few beats. He began to bounce on his toes. "One. Two. Three," he said, and he took off, turning hard to begin his first lap.

The other team looked at one another in shock and confusion; the Fugees looked at one another in relief. As Majok passed behind our bench, I nodded and gave him a quick thumbs-up.

The ref came over to ask if I wanted to send in a substitute.

"No, he'll get back in when he's ready," I said. The Fugees seemed to come on a little stronger then, covering for their teammate as he ran in wide circles around them. A couple of minutes later, Majok stepped back into the game as the Fugees coasted to victory.

The other team was quick to leave. As the Fugees started packing up, I heard the kids begin mumbling, "Where are my shoes?"

I looked to the steps where we usually left our gym shoes when we changed into our cleats. They were all gone. The opposing team had taken off with them.

"They took our shoes!" the boys exclaimed with anger in their voices.

All of a sudden, Majok started laughing.

"They took our shoes," he said. "As if that was going to make them win!"

After a brief silence, someone said, "Coach, they took *your* shoes."

I laughed and looked at Majok. "I'd rather win than keep a pair of shoes," I said. "Plus, mine were a little stinky."

———

There wasn't a lot I could do about Majok's home life, and he was too old for Fugees Academy by the time we started class in the church basement. But coaching Majok taught me a valuable lesson about what kids need to feel safe — and how their behavior can change when they do.

Maybe I was attuned to Majok because I, too, had spent so much of my own life feeling unsafe. Not only did I grow up in a region forever embroiled in war and conflict, but my own safety, as a woman and as a gay woman, was constantly under siege. I knew about honor killings, knew that the police could pull you over and harass you — or worse — just for being a female out on your own. When I got to Smith and found a safe space to be wholly myself, I thrived. But during my senior year, as I worked on my asylum application, my moods were volatile. I punched walls, I yelled at my roommates, I could hardly keep a bite of food in my stomach. The uncertainty — my inability to protect myself — was crushing. Even after I received asylum, I spent years numb and detached, unable to reconcile the catastrophic break that leaving my family and renouncing my Jordanian citizenship represented. I shunned close relationships and genuine emotion and honed a bulletproof bravado.

According to Dr. Bessel van der Kolk, author and expert in the science of trauma, "After trauma the world becomes sharply divided between those who know and those who don't. People who have not shared the traumatic experience cannot be trusted, because they cannot understand it." I don't think it was a coincidence that I did not feel safe again until I met the Fugees, until I was surrounded by people who had been through the same thing. I didn't need my shields anymore, didn't need to explain myself. They understood.

Locking eyes with Majok, reassuring him that I was right there — maybe I instinctually knew how to do that because it was what I had needed the many times I was alone and afraid. This eye-to-eye, heart-to-heart sense of safety would come to define the environment we work tirelessly to cultivate at Fugees Academy. After many years, I would argue that the thing we know more than any other is that for kids to learn and grow they *must* feel safe. No matter what.

We often ask our kids what it is that makes our school different. Over and over, we hear that they feel safe there. That we don't have fights in the school, that no one makes fun of you, and if they do, they probably won't do it again. This desire, this need for safety, isn't unique among refugee students; they aren't the only kids who have experienced trauma. Any average school is full of traumatized youth — children of addicts or abusers, children who have witnessed violence in their neighborhoods or been the victim of it in their home. If there's any doubt that we live in a country full of traumatized kids, consider that prescriptions for pediatric CNS stimulants (the drugs used to treat depression and attention deficit disorders) skyrocketed 483 percent from 1990 to 2015. This trend will likely be exacerbated by the collective trauma of the COVID-19 pandemic.

Most trauma is, at its core, characterized by a loss of control or autonomy. Some of us react by becoming deeply agitated human beings; some of us react by withdrawing deep inside ourselves. But all of us experience changes in our nervous system that hamper our ability to function in a positive way. In short, our fight-or-flight systems have gone haywire. Traumatized kids are often misdiagnosed with learning disabilities or behavioral issues. But treating those symptoms ignores the root of the issue and won't result in authentic progress. "Despite the well-documented effects of anger, fear, and anxiety on the ability to reason, many programs continue to ignore the need to engage the safety system of the brain before trying to promote new ways of thinking," says van der Kolk. You can't medicate or punish trauma out of the body. "For our physiology to calm down, heal, and grow, we need a visceral feeling of safety."

What that means for kids like Majok is that not only do they need to learn coping skills, like counting to ten or running, they also need a consistent and stable environment in which to practice those skills, where they can succeed and mess up and succeed and mess up again knowing that they are surrounded by people who support and love them regardless.

When our students aren't progressing as quickly as we would like or "the way they're supposed to," we know that there are many other factors in play that may have nothing to do with their teacher, their facility with a subject, or their academic potential. Just like Majok's violent episode had nothing to do with that slide tackle, many of our students' challenges are the result of things we can't see or measure: the aftereffects of trauma. Nadine Burke Harris, the surgeon general of California who has researched and written extensively about the long-term effects of childhood adversity, has argued that trauma during the early years of our lives can wreak havoc on lots of systems in the body. "High doses of adversity not only affect brain structure and function, they affect the immune system, hormonal systems, and even the way our DNA is read and transcribed." To patients attempting to heal from these kinds of wounds, she suggests strategies that Fugees Academy has been prioritizing from the beginning: sleep, good nutrition, healthy relationships with peers, and exercise.

The opposite of safety isn't danger — it's uncertainty. All of us function best and feel better when we know what to expect and what is expected of us. When I was growing up, the moments I felt truly safe typically happened on the soccer field or in the dojo when, for one hour, I was the strongest person in the world, punching and kicking through wooden boards. It didn't matter so much that I was good or bad at these sports, what made the difference was the routine, the structure, the opportunity to turn off my anxious mind and just be in my body. Even as I got older, I turned to this coping mechanism often. In the year after my asylum decision, when I was living in the mountains of North Carolina, I ran up and down every hill in sight.

Sports also help our students improve their self-esteem and challenge the preconceived notions that they — and others — have about themselves. A few years ago, I started a cross-country team at our campus in Atlanta. To build the roster, I didn't go for my top athletes; I recruited the students who needed the team the most, the students who were struggling with their confidence. We trained all season, and at every meet, our time dropped. When we finally won a meet, fourteen-year-old Zeinab asked if she could take the trophy home.

"Why?" I asked.

"My mom didn't believe we could win," Zeinab said.

Turns out that Zeinab's mom thought that her daughter should have focused on school, that it was Zeinab's brother who was the athlete. At state finals, Zeinab placed sixth overall and led her team to a first-place finish. But best of all, Zeinab exuded newfound confidence. She realized she was capable of things she (or her family) may not have thought possible.

Not only is daily exercise good for our students' physical health, it also keeps them out of trouble. Instead of riding the bus home to an unstructured, unsupervised afternoon of who knows what, they head out to the field with their friends, a literally and figuratively safe space.

This safe-space structure applies to the school day as well. The best teachers I've known have been the ones whose classes are so regimented that the students can basically run them themselves. This doesn't mean there isn't room for improvisation, creativity, or good surprises; it means there's no room for insecurity, chaos, or bad surprises.

We work hard to create a calm ambiance. We don't have metal detectors, security guards, or locked doors. I believe that if the school looks like a prison the kids will feel like prisoners. Subtle cues — like replacing harsh bells and buzzers with classical music — lower the resting heart rate of the building. And nothing is more comforting to kids or any of us than being surrounded by people who truly know us, a feat we pull off with our incessant community building.

Creating this environment doesn't mean that kids won't act out or break down; sometimes it means the opposite. After all, many of our students are coping with the aftermath of incredible trauma, which often causes persistent anxiety. Making them feel safe sometimes involves letting them express that pain when and how they need to.

A few years ago, a Syrian seventh grader named Musa experienced a panic attack in art class. He was crying and convulsing and speaking only in Arabic. When Musa arrived in my office, escorted by his very concerned teacher, he sobbed, "They're dead. They're all dead. I want to be dead."

I knew what was wrong. I keep news alerts set up on my phone for all the areas our students are from, a way to know what "extra" emotions might be walking into the building each morning. The village where Musa grew up had been bombed the day before. Members of his family, including his beloved grandmother, had been killed.

I scolded myself that I should have checked in with Musa that morning. Bad news out of Syria always brought up memories of my own grandmother and emotions that were difficult to deal with — maybe that's why I hadn't.

"Let's call your parents and get you home," I told Musa, thinking that this would make him feel better. "You don't need to be in school today."

All of a sudden Musa was firm. "No! I don't want to go home. I want to be here. Can I just lie on your couch?" he said, pointing to the small sofa in my office.

"Of course you can," I said.

Musa stayed in my office all day. Sometimes he cried, sometimes he wanted to talk about his family in Syria. Why hadn't the rest of his family been allowed to come to the United States? Why had he been spared and none of them? If this country could save their lives, why didn't it? His grandmother had never hurt anybody; she took care of everyone. I let Musa speak in Arabic, breaking school rules. Sometimes you need the comfort of your mother tongue.

I didn't have answers for Musa. I just listened.

Sometimes Musa was quiet, so I was quiet, too.

At 3:30, Musa rose up off the couch.

"Coach, can I go to practice?"

"Of course you can."

I took Musa home that night and walked him to the door to offer my condolences to his mother.

"*Allah yirhamhun*," I said. *May God bless their souls.* Musa's mom and I stood and looked at each other, tacitly conveying the staggering sorrow of all this senseless death, of how impossible it was to grieve from so far away.

She finally spoke. "We are lucky. That we are alive. That we are here."

I wish our school existed in a vacuum, but it doesn't. No school does. I wish I could stop wars or take away my students' pain, but I can't. No one can. Instead, we build a sense of consistency and safety into every aspect of the school day because to do otherwise would be to ignore how students with trauma learn. We make sure every adult in our school understands trauma but also knows it's not their job to "handle" or fix outbursts on their own.

On November 9, 2016, my phone wouldn't stop vibrating. Texts were coming in from everywhere, from friends and family, and from parents and teachers wondering if we were going to have class that day. Donald Trump had somehow clinched the presidency and his disdain for Muslims and immigrants had been a central part of his winning platform. Our students were scared.

They were listening when Trump pledged to deport the "secret army" of Syrian refugees — most of whom were Muslim — out of the country. They were listening when he said he would "certainly look at" the idea of closing mosques in the United States. They were listening when he made sure to note that the parents of a mass shooter were Muslim immigrants from Afghanistan. "The children of Muslim American parents, they're responsible for a growing number of terrorist attacks," he said. "A number of these immigrants have hostile attitudes."

They heard him loud and clear when he called for a "total and complete shutdown of Muslims entering our country" in December 2015 at a rally in South Carolina. And they heard the roar of the crowd in response.

During the presidential primary campaign, I quickly went from amused to alarmed as Trump's Republican competitors started dropping out of the race. When polls showed Trump gaining ground on Hillary Clinton, I was shocked. Maybe I shouldn't have been; after all, as the coach of an all-refugee soccer team, I often had a front-row seat to the xenophobia that simmers beneath the surface of American life. But how could this message be resonating on such a large scale? How was this kind of talk so acceptable — so welcome — to so many Americans? This didn't feel like the America that had granted me asylum when my survival depended on it.

At first, the kids would make jokes about Trump and try to figure out which group he would target next. But I watched as their bluster quietly melted into worry, and it was difficult for me to reassure them — after all, I felt the same way.

So on that windy morning in November I felt extra helpless. We greeted the students at the door as we always do. Most of them looked distressed; some of them were crying. Their eyes were full of questions. I patted shoulders and leaned into passenger's-seat windows to offer reassurance to parents on their way to work.

"It'll be okay," I said over and over. But I didn't know if that was true.

The school felt like a bubble overinflated with fear and uncertainty. After the kids arrived, I pulled the teachers into a huddle.

"We have to be strong today. Positive. Acknowledge the fear but don't feed into it." A dozen brave faces looked back at me. We decided the best idea was to address the news first thing as a group.

"I know several of you are worried and scared about what happened last night," I began. "And we want to take this time to answer questions you may have."

The questions came rapid-fire.

"Are they going to kick us out?"

"Does America hate us?"

"Should we not go to the mosque?"

"Will we be put on a list?"

"I heard that he will put all Muslims in one place, and no one can stop him."

"Hold on!" I interrupted. I needed to control this narrative before it got out of hand. "I know many of us grew up in places where the presidents and kings had all the power. But the United States is different. We have checks and balances, and a Congress with two houses."

"But the Republicans have it all," someone objected. I noticed the teachers looking at one another nervously.

"That's true, but the president doesn't have all the power; he can't make decisions by himself."

"What do you mean the president doesn't have power?"

"He has power, but it's not the same as back in our countries. He can't decide to go to war."

"He can't?"

"No."

"Can he kick Muslims out?"

"He can't kick citizens out of their own country," I said, immediately regretting my choice of words. Some of our students were citizens, but many had green cards and were not yet eligible for naturalization.

"So he can kick Muslims out if they aren't citizens?"

I swallowed my breath.

That's when I felt William next to me. "Coach, can I say something?" he half whispered.

"Sure," I told him. I was surprised. My staff rarely interrupted me, and William had never wanted to address everyone at once. He was more of a one-on-one guy.

William turned to the students and paused for a moment. "I served this country during a time when America was very divided. A lot of people thought we weren't going to get through it, but we did, and we came out stronger."

The kids didn't say a word. William is a big guy, but suddenly, up there in the front of the room, he looked downright giant, like an offensive lineman, like a bodyguard.

"*No one* is going to come and get you. Because if they do, they will have to go through me. And I am not going to let anyone touch you."

The entire room seemed to sigh with relief. As the kids left the fellowship hall, I noticed more chatter, more smiles. It was as if William's reassurance had resealed our bubble of safety and everyone could breathe again.

If we hadn't gathered to talk that morning, I'm almost certain that there wouldn't have been much learning going on that day or the next. Taking thirty minutes to address the students' concerns head-on — and reminding them that we would protect them — allowed us to reset the pulse. With their heart rates back to normal, the kids could focus.

It takes such small gestures to make kids feel safe, but the ramifications of failing to do so are anything but small. I've learned that the hard way.

It was a September evening in 2015, late in the summer but still relentlessly muggy. I had plenty of work to do — a whole school year to plan. This one would be our first with graduating high school seniors. It should have been a high point, but it didn't feel that way. That spring I had failed to reach my fundraising targets for the first time since founding the school. Everything seemed to be going in the wrong direction.

But the students remained the bright spot, the motivation to keep going. They had just wrapped up their summer performance of *Annie* and had done an incredible job. They blew me away.

Emily wasn't home yet, so dinner could wait. I grabbed a beer from the fridge and collapsed on the couch, flipping the TV to the six o'clock news and half listening while I returned emails and texts on my phone. Local news, much milder than world news but still a good way to keep tabs on the neighborhood, was something I watched in order to decompress. My ears scanned the noise for just a couple of words: *Clarkston, Stone Mountain, DeKalb County.* Otherwise, I tuned out.

I remember I was reaching for my drink when I saw the face on the television. My heart sputtered; my throat tightened. It was Majok.

A gun-toting man, the news anchor said.

A domestic dispute.

The video showed police storming into a run-down apartment building.

Shot himself.

Apparent suicide.

Apparent suicide.

Apparent suicide.

Majok had been in and out of my life for the past six years. In and out of jail, too. Disappearing and reappearing on the soccer field. Sometimes he would watch from the top of the hill next to the field, waving at us from above. Sometimes he would run down and join us. I had made small breakthroughs with him, but Majok always seemed to teeter on the precipice of something I couldn't pull him back from. In 2005, when Majok was thirteen, his father committed suicide. Before he did, he scribbled a note for his children to find. "It's all your fault," someone told me it said. Majok tumbled off the edge.

I hadn't seen him for a few months when I learned in 2013 that there was a warrant out for his arrest for armed robbery. Majok was eighteen. I didn't have his number anymore but took some comfort in knowing that if he needed me he knew exactly where to find me — on the field with the Fugees every afternoon. Unfortunately, the police were well aware of that, too.

One afternoon a squad car pulled into the parking lot. Moments later, two officers emerged and plodded onto the field. They wanted to know if I had seen Majok.

"No, I haven't seen him in a while," I said.

"We need to speak to him. Do you have any way of reaching him?"

"I don't," I said. I turned to my players and asked if they had seen Majok or could reach him. I already knew the answer, and I was hoping to get on with our practice. A bunch of heads shook no. Even if they knew where Majok was, they were not going to tell a cop. These young men did not trust the police.

The officers returned to their car but didn't leave. We started practice, running laps before spreading out for push-ups and sit-ups. I was counting out loud when I looked to the top of the hill and saw Majok, unmistakable with his long arms and long legs, peeling off a shoe with one hand, a cleat in the other. As we made eye contact, he smiled, probably waiting for my finger to circle the air — latecomers run extra. Instead, he got a terse shake of the head. He looked confused, hurt almost, then he saw the cop car.

He got it. He ran.

The cops didn't notice but my team did.

"If you know how to get ahold of him," I told them, "tell him to turn himself in. This isn't going to go away. And if he wants to talk, tell him I'll be at the field early tomorrow."

Sure enough, Majok showed up at the field the next day looking thin and tired.

"I can't have the police coming to the field trying to arrest you in front of the team."

"I'm sorry, Coach."

"Tell me what you did and I can help. The longer you wait, the worse it's going to be."

"Nothing, Coach. There's nothing you can do. I'll go in." He toed the dirt with his sneaker.

"Majok, I can help you. You don't have to do this alone."

"I'll go in," he repeated before turning and walking away.

To this day, I don't know if Majok turned himself in or if he was eventually arrested.

Three years later, a bigger, more muscular Majok showed up to the field. His arms were adorned with tattoos and he had a button-down tucked into his pants. I wondered if all my lectures about dressing like a gentleman had finally paid off.

"Hey, Coach," Majok said with a wide smile. "You remember me?"

"Of course I do! When did you get this old?"

"I'm only twenty!" Majok's face had matured, but I could still see all that mischief and heart. A little of that old darkness remained, but there was something else, too — something settled and calm.

"I'm a dad, Coach."

"A dad? No way!"

"Two boys. Four and two. I hear you have a daughter."

"I do. She's one."

"Maybe she will marry my son."

"Only if he is more handsome than you," I teased.

"Coach — he is. Look." Majok pulled his phone out of his pocket and scrolled through the photos. When he turned it around, there he was on the screen holding two beautiful children, the three of them beaming.

"They look so much like you!"

"I'm a good dad," he said, as if he were trying to convince me.

I kept looking at the photo, wanting to memorize the happiness I saw in it. Wanting to believe Majok's life had worked out.

"I'm a good dad," he repeated. "Not like —"

"I know you're a good dad because you're a good person. Sometimes those of us with less-than-great parents turn out to be great parents ourselves."

Majok nodded and put his phone back in his pocket.

"Is there a wife or a girlfriend?" I asked.

"Kinda," Majok said, wrinkling his nose.

"Kinda? She'd better adore you. She doesn't know how lucky she is."

He showed up to the field sporadically that spring. Once, he brought his sons to practice and they watched as he helped me coach a group of younger kids.

"This is the best thing that will ever happen to you," he told them. "No one will love you the way Coach does. Don't screw it up."

But by the summer, Majok stopped coming around. A few months later, he was dead.

The newscast had moved on to some other story. My phone buzzed in my hand. It was Lewis.

"You watch the news, Coach?" he texted.

"Yes."

"Majok."

"I'll meet you at the field."

Lewis was there. So were Assif and Sulayman. Elijah showed up not long after. We mostly just sat in silence. A few more kids trickled in, one with a soccer ball. We started kicking it around, running up and down the field. Running and running and running. No matter how far or how long we ran, our hearts would never stop hurting.

I no longer watch the local news. A few weeks after Majok's death, another former player was shot in a drug deal gone wrong. Then another was arrested. Now every murder and death of a young Black man is a reminder of Majok; every face on the screen represents a coach, a family, a community, and a nation that has failed them.

CATCHING UP
FROM FAR BEHIND

'M NORMALLY NOT ONE FOR CONFERENCES, ALL THAT SIT-
ting and having to engage in small talk. But the 2013 Building a
Grad Nation Summit was different. There was a powerhouse
lineup — then Secretary of Education Arne Duncan, General Colin
Powell, and former First Lady Laura Bush — and Fugees Academy
was on the cusp of accreditation victory. I was ready to soak in the
brilliance, to be inspired. To see how others were doing it and make
connections with colleagues from nonprofits and big school districts. I had been counting down the days for weeks.

Almost immediately, I knew my expectations were off by a mile.
Speaker after speaker talked about the importance of early learning and intervention, about predictors of student success — and failure. Maybe others heard the inspirational parts or the words of hope
from these visionaries, but all I could hear was doom and gloom.
They spoke of students like mine, kids well into their adolescence
who were raised by illiterate parents, kids who had experienced
poverty or trauma or violence.

Highly unlikely to graduate.
Brains are 90 percent developed by age six.
Will drop out.

I left the conference room with a leaden feeling in my stomach. What were we doing? Were we naive? Foolish, even? We had put all that work into accreditation — would it even matter? All of these data points, according to the experts assembled for the conference, could mean only one thing — a dead end for our Fugees.

I paced the long blocks of D.C. trying to shake off the anger and doubt I was feeling. The sky was stark blue; fall's first chill hung in the shadows. Those were *my students* the speakers were talking about. Well, kind of. My students had actually experienced far worse than most American kids. Famine, disease, bombs, families slaughtered and raped in front of them. Their parents weren't just illiterate, many of them had no formal education at all. Some of their parents had been killed.

A bench appeared and I collapsed on it, crossing my arms over my chest. I thought of Jiddo, a fourteen-year-old from South Sudan. His story was a collage of these risk factors. He had lived most of his young life in a refugee camp, had gone days without food and water. With no access to health care, his mother had died there. Only when Jiddo and his surviving family members had made it to the United States did he pick up his first book — he was nine years old by then. The book was written in a language he could not speak. Because of these experiences, according to the data, Jiddo had no chance of graduating.

But what about what the data did not capture? I suddenly thought. What about how Jiddo had become a leader on the soccer team, had scored hat trick after hat trick? That he had been so hungry to learn to read that it had taken him only three years to get caught up with most kids his age? Where did all of this factor into the dire predictions? No, these people didn't know Jiddo, so they couldn't possibly know what I knew — that he would graduate in three years. Sitting on that bench in the shade of some low-slung federal building, I *knew*.

Jiddo would succeed not *despite* his lived experiences but *because* of them. After all, what's so intimidating about learning to read and do math when you have already lived through the worst? If you survived hunger and war and profound loss, the challenge of graduating high school was surmountable. We needed to shift the way we looked at our students, to see their lived experiences as assets, not deficits. Leaving our countries and starting a new life makes us stronger, not weaker. Learning a new language makes us smarter, and navigating two cultures makes us more compassionate.

I wanted to run back into the conference hall and tell everyone about Jiddo. I wanted to say that the statistics on the slides were telling only half the story. I respect science and value hard-won research but not if they give us an excuse to quit. The conclusion to be drawn from the data was not that our students wouldn't succeed but that we had been doing something fundamentally wrong. The conclusion should have been that it was time for a massive change.

When we started Fugees Academy, our curriculum looked like everyone else's. We had math, English, social studies, the occasional music and art class. The only thing that really set us apart was that everyone played soccer each afternoon. Over and over, most of the students told me that they only came to school so they could play soccer afterward. They got to play soccer, they felt safe in our school, but they were still struggling. How could they learn history and science if they could hardly read? They were always behind, always gasping for breath.

In short, we had designed a school to fit into the American system, a system that had consistently failed our students. But schools shouldn't be about systems; they should be about students. So we adapted. We redesigned the school to put our students' strengths and their needs at the heart of everything we do.

———

At our Atlanta campus, my office sat directly above the school's music room. In our drafty old building, air and sound traveled at will, so I had a front-row (top-floor?) seat to each one of Mr. Jason's classes. Many days I'd resort to headphones to drown out the happy cacophony of kids learning "The Star-Spangled Banner," the latest Taylor Swift song, or the greatest hits of the Motown era.

But no matter what the repertoire was for that day, Mr. Jason's classes always started the same way: with the scales. Even when he was alone in his classroom getting ready for the school day, Jason — an internationally renowned conductor — began his *own* practice with the scales. Those basic notes always stirred some nostalgia in me. It was the same way my own music classes had started in elementary school; the same way Fräulein Maria had taught the von Trapp kids to sing: "Let's start at the very beginning, a very good place to start."

Jason is an exceptional musician and teacher. The students adore him. When he arrived at Fugees Academy not long after the conference in D.C., we were desperate for a music teacher. All the candidates I had interviewed had been lackluster, teachers who seemed to think music class was nothing more than a sing-along. A day before that year's orientation, Jason sat down in front of my desk for his interview. He was charming and funny. I had a good feeling about him. When he started talking about music, that feeling turned into certainty.

Jason told me about his mentor, Virginia, a first-generation Chinese immigrant who had been his sixth-grade teacher. Jason loved Virginia's class so much that about halfway through the school year he decided that he wanted to learn the piano and he wanted his beloved music teacher to teach him. Virginia was a busy middle school teacher, so she turned him down. It was only after he theatrically jumped on the hood of her car to demonstrate how desperate he was to learn that she agreed to tutor him in piano every day after school. The mentorship quickly expanded beyond music; Jason told me that Virginia helped him stay safe in his rough Philadelphia neighborhood and made sure that he got into college (and majored in music). To this day, they still talk on the phone every Sunday night.

When he was a teenager, the piano had been for Jason an escape — from his everyday stresses and his very station in life. Sometimes he even skipped school to play piano. He was certain that if it weren't for his mentor and his music he wouldn't have made it out of his neighborhood.

Jason's story resonated with me as a person and a principal. That he had broken into a predominantly white space as a Black conductor made me feel confident that he understood the challenges our students were confronting and how to overcome them. But I didn't want my gut or the clock to decide whether or not I hired Jason, so I asked him to teach a sample lesson that day, a day when we were making academic assessments of our new students — new to the school and new to the country.

"Now?" he asked.

"Now," I said.

"How many kids?"

"Twenty."

"Is there a piano downstairs?"

"No."

"Are there any instruments?"

"No."

"Okay! Let's do it!"

What I saw that day in the music room was nothing short of magic. In thirty minutes, Jason taught the kids how to count off a beat. It didn't matter that most of them couldn't understand English — they all were soon clapping and smiling and utterly focused on Jason. Each time they got something right, Jason stepped it up another level before going right back to the beginning again. When Jason was finished, none of the kids were talking about the tests they had just taken or the new school year that was about to start. They were all clapping and trying to create their own beats.

For a final check, I needed to call Jason's references. I called Virginia. This ended up being the reverse of any reference check I have ever done. She interviewed me, asking about the school, how much autonomy Jason would have, and what instruments the students would play. I told her that we didn't have any instruments yet but that in one year we would have enough for everyone. She made me promise that this was true.

"The kids all need to learn how to play," she advised me.

"Yes, ma'am, I totally agree."

"It's as important as math or English."

I had no idea how we would afford our music program, but that wasn't going to stop me from starting one.

These days, our students take music and visual arts at least four times a week throughout their middle school years. These subjects don't just provide the students an alternative language to express themselves in while they learn English, they also help them learn English. Singing is a low-pressure way to practice words, tone, inflection — and poise. (A great example of this phenomenon is the seventies supergroup ABBA, some of whose members could sing chart-topping hits in English but couldn't actually speak it.) The arts provide a multisensory experience that allows students to *see* and *feel* the language they're learning. The prevailing stereotype is that artists are absentminded or flighty. In reality — and in our school — artists are as disciplined as athletes, so they fit right in.

In a choir or on a soccer team, everyone works together while honing their own talent; mediocrity is rooted out through consistent performance with rigorous standards; and no matter who or how old you are, you start with the fundamentals. We all want to be a superstar, to be a power forward, a spelling bee champion, a black belt.

But Mr. Miyagi was right — wax on, wax off. Hard work, focus, and repetition.

Nowhere is this more obvious (or more controversial) than in learning to read. From the beginning, Fugees Academy has relied on phonics — sounding out letters or groups of letters that make up words — to teach our students to read. In a traditional setting, phonics is used in kindergarten and first grade if at all. In our population, phonics is almost always necessary in middle school when new speakers of English are still learning the basic elements of the language. While it may seem jarring to watch a twelve-year-old learn how to round his lips into a *sh* sound or point his tongue into a *th* sound, these are the indispensable first steps of becoming a reader, especially for non-native speakers, some of whom have never made or heard these sounds in their home language.

As a soccer coach, I have always found that this approach makes perfect sense. I would never teach my players advanced skills without first teaching them the feel of the ball on the foot. That first touch is the basis of everything: passing, receiving, shooting. For a good player, touch is muscle memory, but it's never a given. That's why we practice it every time we're on the field. Watch a professional soccer team warming up — they're doing the same drills despite being at the apex of their profession. We look at reading in the same way. To learn the skill, you first need to learn the building blocks. Then, even as your understanding becomes more sophisticated, returning to the building blocks again and again solidifies that muscle memory, unburdening you to become confident and creative. Just like Tom Brady and Serena Williams still spend hours a day on the fundamentals. Just like my best players still practice footwork. Just like Jason plays the scales.

Many well-intentioned people have advocated for the idea that literacy is a natural process, meaning that if you surround a child with books they will eventually learn to read. This is called the whole language approach, and it prioritizes the physical practice of reading, listening, and speaking, and suggests that students will just "get it" if they spend enough time doing it. But years of research have found that reading is not a natural process, especially for non-native speakers. If you're skeptical, buy a few children's books written in Swahili. Place them around your home. Spend lots of time flipping through them. See how long it takes you to learn to read Swahili.

Reading is about so much more than sounding out words. It's about perceiving context and deriving meaning. But students can't reach those advanced echelons of literacy without the early stepping-stones of deciphering.

Or in the immortal words of those von Trapp refugees, "When you know the notes to sing, you can sing most anything."

This is a strategy we apply across academic subjects, including math and science. We start at the beginning. Still, for many years, we have faced resistance — from teachers who didn't feel comfortable teaching nursery rhymes to preteens and from the students who quite often have been mocked or infantilized for being so behind. Like most kids, they have a strong desire to appear "normal."

I remember a math class I was sitting in on at the beginning of a school year. The kids were technically in sixth grade, but for many of them, this was their first formal instruction.

"This says 'grade 1a,'" one of the boys said, looking down at his new textbook.

"What do you mean?" I asked, confused.

"The book says 'grade 1a,' but we're in sixth grade."

"Do you know everything in this book?" I directed the question at the entire class.

No one said a word.

I flipped the book open to a random page. I posed a few of the easier equations out loud.

Again, no one said a word.

"Has anyone ever taught you this stuff?"

There were a few mumbled noes.

"So how do you expect to know it?"

"But this is for little kids!" the original boy protested. "We aren't little kids."

"Let's say I went to Ethiopia and I had to speak Amharic. Would you start me with a big book? Or would you start me at the beginning?"

"At the beginning."

"Does that mean I am stupid?"

The kids shook their heads.

"No, it just means that I need to work harder than most people my age to learn. We believe you can get through grades one through three in one year and grades four and five in the next. Because you will work so hard. Because you are so smart and so strong. And by the time you get to eighth grade, you'll be ready for high school."

"What if we can't?" a student asked.

"What if we fail?" said another.

I sensed that the real reason they were objecting to their "little kid" textbook was the fear that they wouldn't be able to achieve all that we were setting out for them to achieve.

"If you fail, you'll repeat the grade. You can't go to the next level until you know the one before it or you'll get to high school and you won't know how to read or write or do math."

This exchange sounds so simple, I know. But this idea — that kids must master the material of one grade before being passed onto the next — is anything but a given in American schools. My earliest players taught me that. Lewis had made it through three grades even though his teachers *knew* he couldn't read. How many adults had failed him in that time? Our students may come to us in sixth grade, but it's still our responsibility to make sure they know everything they should have learned in first through fifth. The proverbial buck has to stop somewhere.

Social promotion—placing kids in grades based on their age, not their skill level—is an insidious phenomenon, one that takes two distinct forms. It may be an act of "compassion" by teachers and administrators who fret about breaking a kid's spirit. Or it may be an expression of surrender, of giving up, of saying, "It's too late and it's too hard."

Every time a teacher doesn't hold a student accountable to spare their feelings or build their confidence, the student knows. And the message that student receives is "I don't think you can do this" or worse, "I don't care if you can or not." It is not hyperbole to say that avoiding the momentary discomfort of a conflict or a tough conversation causes long-term damage in the student's life. It also degrades the value of a degree. Every smiley face, every passing grade that is given to subpar student work is part of the system that blocks students from being able to develop prospects beyond dead-end minimum-wage jobs (at best). It might seem, in the moment, that passing a student who is not yet performing at grade level is the kind thing to do, but really we are guaranteeing that the students we take pity on now, the students we give sympathy grades to, will be the same ones handing out orders from drive-through windows twenty years in the future.

While today social promotion tends to be pervasive among low-income and minority populations, the practice was actually forwarded by progressive education reformers like John Dewey in the early half of the last century. Dewey thought the emotional impact of holding students back was more damaging than being academically ill-equipped for the next grade. Applied today, this is a shortsighted, paternalistic perspective, one that ignores the emotional (not to mention the social and financial) impact of adult illiteracy on both individuals and their communities.

What we understand now is that teachers' expectations of their students have a material effect on their performance. A study carried out by researchers at Johns Hopkins University and American University concluded that a teacher's high expectations line up with high outcomes because, in short, "high expectations about a student . . . translate into more school and teacher resources being devoted to the student or more effort on the part of the student." It is worrying that these same researchers and many others have found that white teachers have lower expectations for students of color. If we expect our students to succeed, it's more likely that they will, and students who are traditionally seen (and may see themselves) as lost causes need our confidence even more.

At Fugees Academy, our insistence on rigor and mastery is our way of demonstrating just how much we believe in our students. It would be lazy — and, quite frankly, racist — to have lower expectations and standards for them because of their barriers, to assume they don't have the capacity to learn everything they need to by the end of high school, to accept that theirs will be a fate defined by mediocrity. Giving our sixth-grade students sixth-grade textbooks that they couldn't possibly understand wouldn't be compassionate or a vote of confidence. It would be setting them up for failure. Teaching them that there is no shame in being a beginner and that acquiring a complex skill requires starting with the basics — in soccer, music, or reading — is a way to show belief in our students. This is true not just for our population but for all children — not just in our school but in every school.

Designing an academic program for kids who are arriving at their education with a significant deficit to make up isn't simple. A big part of our work involves rejecting another aspect of the same white paternalism inherent in social promotion: books from only the Western canon, word problems with only American names, classrooms that don't prioritize our community's contributions and values.

At Fugees Academy, we are constantly searching for ways to make lessons and learning materials relevant to all races and ethnicities represented in the school. Just as it's important for students to see adults who look and sound like them, they also need to see themselves in the books they read, the math problems they solve, and the songs they sing.

A few years ago, sixth graders Samia, Gaston, and Nahom were huddled over a book during reading period, the sun shining through the window behind them.

"You ask her," I heard Gaston tell Samia. Samia shook her head adamantly.

Nahom seemed to take a big breath. "Coach?" he asked. "What is a *dick*?"

"Excuse me?"

"What is a dick? It's here in the book." He pointed to the open pages.

"Let me see what book you're reading." We had received donated boxes of books, and I hadn't gone through all of them before the kids began eagerly choosing their own. I knelt down next to the students' table.

"It says *Dick and Jane*," Nahom said.

I laughed, mostly out of relief. "Oh! It's a name. Dick is a name."

"A name?" Now the kids all looked confused.

"Yes, just like Nahom, or Samia, or Gaston."

I took a seat and started reading the book out loud, only this time I changed the names to ones that would be familiar to them. This is a skill I have honed over forty years since my early tutoring days: trying to make things more relevant to students by changing names and settings and using a lot (*a lot*) of soccer analogies. For my daughters, stories about mommy and daddy have recently become stories about mommy and mama.

Even though I was using new names, the kids were unimpressed. "This is boring," Gaston said.

"It's an old book," I said.

"So Dick is a name," Samia said, looking satisfied with this new knowledge.

"Hold on, Samia. It's a name, but it's almost never used anymore."

"Do you know a Dick?" he asked.

"Um. Not really." I knew what I had to do. Our students too often use American slang out of context and are accidentally rude or obscene. They watch something on TV or hear it on the playground, then use the word to try to fit in. I knew how this "dick" thing was going to play out if I didn't step in.

"It also has a bad meaning," I said.

"A name has a bad meaning?"

I understood their confusion. Names — their stories and their meanings — were a highly regarded part of their cultures.

"Yes. It also means 'penis,' a boy's private parts."

Six wide eyes looked back at me.

Like my students, I had no interest in books I couldn't relate to.

One afternoon when I was in the first grade, I was visiting my grandmother after school. Still struggling with all-English instruction, I was feeling tired and frustrated, and she sensed it.

"How was school today?" she asked.

"It was okay, but everyone is smarter than I am."

"Why do you say that?"

"The teacher read a story and they all laughed at some parts and got scared at other parts, but I didn't understand why."

"What was the story about, Lamloom?" she asked, stroking my hair.

"It was about a red jacket. And the red jacket went to visit a grandmother, but it wasn't allowed to talk to anyone on the way. And then a dog wanted to eat the jacket. But jackets don't talk and dogs don't eat jackets! I just don't think I am very smart."

My grandmother looked at me sympathetically. "Why don't I tell you the story of Leila and the wolf?" she said.

I loved that story and I loved when my grandmother told it. It wasn't in a book she read from — in Arabic, the oral tradition is strong. I grew up listening to my grandmother tell stories, some true, some fables, many wildly embellished.

"Yes, please, tell me again."

"*Kan ya makan, fi kadeem al zaman*," she began. *Once upon a time*. That's the way all our stories began. The storyteller would say, "*Kan ya makan*," and the listeners would reply, "*Fi kadeem al zaman*."

"There was a girl called Leila who wore a red hat. One day, her mother asked her to take food to her grandmother's house but warned her not to speak to anyone until she got there. On the way, Leila meets a wolf. The wolf asks Leila to play, but she refuses. She says she is going to her grandmother's house with some food. The wolf says they should gather flowers to give to the grandmother."

My grandmother paused and looked at me, waiting to see if I understood.

"Little Red Riding Hood is a name!" I exclaimed. "The jacket is Leila!"

This is a simple example but one that demonstrates what is lost when cultural barriers aren't considered. Little Red Riding Hood was inaccessible to my Arabic-oriented brain, so I missed out on the lessons of the fairy tale. I was too focused on a talking jacket to appreciate the moral of the story. Nahom, Samia, and Gaston couldn't practice their reading skills because of one confounding word. I speak English with native fluency, but to this day, when I don't understand an idea or concept in English, I plug in Arabic names or places to light up different parts of my brain. I've been doing this my entire life.

Zaretta Hammond, the self-described "former writing teacher turned equity freedom fighter," is best known for her book *Culturally Responsive Teaching and the Brain*. In a recent workshop she hosted for school leaders and teachers, Hammond shared an observation about the term "culturally responsive." She described — with apparent frustration—fielding emails and comments from well-intentioned folks seeking a workshop or a reading list or a curriculum recommendation so they can "do CRT." When the adults who have power in a school or in a school system try to change an aspect of their programming to be more culturally responsive, they often do so with a sense of urgency, a desire for action. Urgency and action are fine, but if we want things to change, we have to admit to ourselves that our schools wouldn't be failing so many kids if it were as easy as good intentions, a workshop, and a reading list.

Hammond's book details neuroscience principles that explain how vital it is to commit to a practice of centering *the children we are actually teaching* in our teaching. CRT incorporates much of what I've discussed in previous chapters: a focus on community, strong relationships with students' families, a diverse staff, caring adults, and high expectations for all students. It also stresses the importance of a culturally diverse curriculum, one that integrates ideas related to the students' backgrounds and cultures. Curriculums that aren't adapted in this way are not only alienating for students but also discouraging, disheartening, and confusing. That said, there is no shortcut, no way to copy and paste. There is no "culturally responsive" curriculum that a school can just plug in and play. To be truly culturally responsive, we need to make sure our reading lists and story problems reflect the lived experiences of the students in our buildings, but that has to be the icing on the cake, the natural extension of long, slow, respectful relationship and community building. Otherwise it's just icing.

We face challenges when choosing books about the refugee or immigrant experience. Too many books focus on depressing aspects of our identity, and too few actually celebrate the multitudes we contain. Trust me, refugees don't want to constantly read about how shitty their lives are. We want to read books that highlight our complexities and our dynamism, ones that don't lump us all together into the same huddled mass. We get enough of that in real life.

———

"I want everyone in this classroom to feel seen, safe, and comfortable," I said. I was sitting in a chair in front of Mr. Frank's ninth-grade world history class to help with damage control. When students had entered their classroom earlier that morning, they had been greeted by a new feature adorning the walls: flags from their countries of origin. Mr. Frank had meant well; he wanted to show the kids that he valued their heritage, wanted to make them feel at home. What he had failed to consider was the complexity of what these flags represented.

He had appeared breathless and frantic, talking a mile a minute in the doorway of my office, summoning me to help him deescalate a mounting conflict between two Syrian students. I followed him back across the hall and immediately saw what the problem was. The Syrian flag on the wall — the one with red on the top (the official flag of these students' home country now claimed by the Assad regime) — was on display, but the opposition's flag — the one with the green on top — was nowhere to be seen. What one student took as a symbol of national pride, the other took as a reminder of the state-sponsored brutality that had decimated his neighborhood and forced him and his family to flee their home. To say this was complicated is an understatement.

I laid the ground rules for a discussion right then and there. I insisted that the students speak from a place of personal truth and rephrase statements that might be perceived as attacks. Everyone, I said, needed to listen carefully for evidence of common ground. Nobody wants to leave home, I reminded the students. Everyone processes differently. Anger, blame, and rhetoric are to be expected, and we have to plan accordingly.

"I guess I shouldn't have put up the flags," Mr. Frank said to me later. I disagreed. The flags in and of themselves were not the problem, and they might even be a nice thing to have up on the wall.

But in this case — as in so many others — we have to back up a few steps, slow down, and think about the process as much as — if not more than — we think about end results. Really think about the students, how our actions, even (especially) the most well-intentioned ones, could be interpreted differently than what we foresee. Maybe Mr. Frank should have started by telling his students that he wanted them to feel seen, safe, and comfortable. Maybe he should have asked them to identify the flag they see as their own.

It isn't cultural responsiveness when the cultures included don't speak for themselves and are explained and viewed from the white perspective instead. This approach cannot be just a feel-good gesture; it must come from the inside out, with students' values, outlooks, and experiences fully understood and centered. When done right, this work is a way of identifying and building on the cognitive framework the students already have. For example, many of our students come from cultures that place an emphasis on the common good over individual success — part of our job is to find learning materials and techniques that harness that value to improve their academic performance. I often say to our students that our team is only as strong as our weakest player, that when one of us is suffering we are all suffering. It is our responsibility to take care of one another. The kids seem to take this to heart.

In our tutoring sessions, our older students help younger ones; when a student is absent, the kids who live nearby go knock on their door; if a student shows up to school with dirty clothes on, someone always has a handful of quarters and directions to the laundromat. The students know they are part of something bigger, and it's not only the teachers and adults who are taking care of them but also their classmates.

Self-esteem and being seen are a vital part of how we interpret cultural responsiveness at Fugees Academy. But the end goal is about rigor, about mastery, and about preparing the student to succeed outside of school whether we get there by teaching phonics to teenagers, taking a page out of ABBA's book, or saying goodbye forever to Dick and Jane.

Our overriding obligation to our students — no matter what the data may say about their potential — is to believe they can succeed and give them all the tools to make that happen.

Three years after the conference in D.C., I handed Jiddo a diploma. As I shook his hand, I felt so proud — of the work he had done, of the work his teachers had done, and that his degree represented high standards, a strong education, and a ticket to a successful future.

REDEFINING SUCCESS

SAFIULLAH WAS AMONG OUR VERY FIRST COHORT OF students at Fugees Academy. He was whip smart and charismatic, a young Afghan boy whose family had fled from the Taliban. Back then, our strategy was just to catch the boys up to their grade level then mainstream them into another school. After three years in our program, Safiullah applied to and was admitted to an elite private high school in Buckhead, the epicenter of affluence in the Atlanta area. At his new school, Safiullah continued to excel. He earned good grades and was captain of the soccer team. In the spring of his senior year, he was accepted to American University to study economics. He graduated in four years.

I used to tell this story all the time. I've told it to countless funders, donors, and board members. I've told it to students and faculty. It makes everyone feel good. But it doesn't make me feel good anymore.

Safiullah was a star student; he's what every teacher wanted. He worked hard and advanced rapidly, but his circumstances were different from the rest of his class. His parents were literate, and he had some formal education back in Afghanistan. His bilingual brain was rewiring itself at a faster clip than our other students' because he could read and write in Farsi while his peers couldn't recognize any alphabet. His progress compared to his classmates was meteoric — and it made us feel great. His success was our success. His teachers spent one-on-one time with him, teaching him algebra while the rest of his class was learning long division. When Safiullah got accepted to that elite school at the end of our three-year program, we celebrated openly even as the other five students matriculated back to the subpar schools of their district. They had also shown incredible growth — performing six or seven grade levels above where they had started. But it wasn't good enough to get into any of the area's private schools on full scholarship.

This was our failure: teaching to the top and neglecting to consider the impact that this had on the other students.

Safiullah kept in touch as he navigated the privileged world he was now a part of. I watched as the young man I had known — the earnest Muslim who always ordered a Filet-O-Fish (in order to keep halal) while his teammates ate cheeseburgers, who attended mosque with his father regularly, who was super protective of his younger sister — transformed into a prep school kid who visited the Fugees' field in his girlfriend's white Range Rover, the girlfriend he wouldn't introduce to his parents out of embarrassment or fear or both. The outside world would surely view Safiullah's story as a success: he had assimilated. But I knew it was more complicated than that. Rejecting your culture, your identity, to fit someone else's version of success was not a triumph, it was a tragedy. *Would he ever truly be comfortable with himself?* I wondered.

Nine years after we started the school, our moment of truth arrived. The college acceptance letters for our first graduating high school class were in their hands. Finally, a tangible indicator of proof that our students had succeeded, that our school had succeeded. At least that's what I thought.

All three of our graduates were accepted to Georgia Perimeter College, the area's community college. This would be their plan B.

Haben was the first to get an acceptance letter from a four-year college, a liberal arts school in the southwest corner of the state. He was thrilled. We were thrilled. I asked Haben to bring all of his paperwork to my office so we could go over the financial details together.

After a few quiet minutes squinting at the numbers, Haben finally said what we both were thinking.

"Why would they even accept me? I can't go." In spite of a ten-thousand-dollar scholarship, the loans he would be required to take out each year amounted to his mother's annual salary — twenty-five thousand a year.

"Let me see what I can do. I know some people at the school — maybe they can do better on the scholarships."

"You shouldn't have to beg, Coach."

That seemed to be my job lately. Begging. Showing everyone what we could do and what we had done. Haben's comment got to me. I started to wonder: Was I thrilled because Haben got into college or because Haben's getting into college would make it easier for us to raise money? Had I spent so many years begging that I had lost sight of what I was begging for? What would this hundred-thousand-dollar criminology degree do for Haben? How many years would it take for him to pay off that debt?

And the FAFSA process had been jarring for us, too. We had helped students fill out these application forms for student financial aid, which are intimidating and confusing to many of their families, and this process felt like applying for food stamps — proving how poor you were and that you couldn't afford the astronomical price of college (as if anyone could). Just like food stamps, the resulting aid seemed designed to make you feel grateful but keep you living in poverty. To make the dream of college seem possible while encouraging mere teenagers to yoke themselves with crippling debt.

"How did you do this, Coach?" Haben asked.

"I, um, I was extremely lucky. I didn't have to take out loans."

Haben's face lit up in amazement. "Full scholarship? For being smart or for soccer?"

"Neither," I said, embarrassed. "My parents paid for it."

"All of it?"

"All of it."

"Wow." Haben's face registered a different kind of amazement.

I wanted to tell him that college was cheaper back then, but in relation to income, it wasn't. I wanted to tell him that my parents really sacrificed to make it work, but they didn't. It was sheer privilege and luck. That was the difference between Haben and me — not our grades, or our heart, or our ambition. Luck.

I knew that Haben's mother — a single woman raising three kids — didn't have the money for college, and I knew that Haben wouldn't ask her for it if she did. Not one of our students would. Many of them were reaching the age when it was expected that they would start supporting and providing for their parents.

"So what would you do if you were me?"

I knew what Haben needed most was honesty, but that didn't make what I had to tell him any easier.

"I wouldn't go."

"You wouldn't go?"

"No. Not unless I could get it down to a number that I could work to pay off each summer. Or I would go to Georgia Perimeter and transfer in two years."

Haben had walked into my office radiating pride and excitement; now he looked deflated and sad.

"You've accomplished something big here. Your mother will still be very proud of you."

"She doesn't even know what college is," Haben said. "She just wants me to go."

It was true; many refugee parents aren't quite sure what happens on an American college campus, but they have been told — and believe, like the majority of our society — that college is the only way for their children to be successful.

I had to have a similar talk with the other two students, each of whom had been accepted to a handful of third-tier private colleges. As dispiriting as these conversations were, they didn't compare to the regret I had been wrestling with for months. My push for college at any cost had been even more damaging to at least one of my students than the shock of the hundred-thousand-dollar loan.

There should have been four graduates. But in February of that year, Tesfay had dropped out. Six years after he had started at Fugees Academy and three months shy of graduation, we lost him. So close to the finish line. At first, I couldn't make sense of it; I thought we had given Tesfay everything he needed to succeed. He loved soccer and was a deadly left wing; other teams underestimated him because of his small size. We never had attendance issues with him; his parents and older brother were supportive. The high school dropout rate is high among Eritrean refugees, and they didn't want him to be another statistic.

Tesfay was one of the kids who told me that if it wasn't for soccer — and sometimes music class or his construction elective — he wouldn't bother with school. But he knew he needed a high school diploma, and everyone in his circle was rooting for him.

But maybe we were rooting for him a little too aggressively. Looking back now, I see that all the pressure we put on our graduating seniors must have made Tesfay feel inadequate and unseen. We were dedicating so much time and energy to SAT prep, admission essays, and FAFSA forms that no one interpreted Tesfay's F in English his senior year as the red flag that it was. He had never failed a class before.

It was my fault. I needed these young men to go to college. I needed them to finish college. They were our ticket — not only to more funding but also to proving that our model could work so we could provide these same opportunities for other refugee kids. Our school—like all schools—would be measured by our graduation rates, college acceptance rates, and matriculation into college. I did not stop to think what kind of weight I was putting on the students' shoulders. I did not stop to truly appreciate their expectation-defying improvement. I did not stop to interrogate the dominant narrative that says that a college acceptance letter is the ultimate arbiter of worth.

I had learned to think differently when I was broke and washing dishes in North Carolina. For the first time in my life, I wasn't on the top looking down, I was on the bottom looking up. And I began to notice every working person—the guy mowing the grass on the side of the road, the grocery store manager, the line cook. I wondered about their backgrounds, their salaries, their job security. I wondered if they were happy, if their needs were being met. In short, I began to see that different circumstances necessitated different choices and produced varying levels of fulfillment.

But that was then. I had forgotten those lessons, and I had not fully learned the lesson that Safiullah had taught me.

In every way he could, Tesfay was telling me that he did not want to go to college, but I wasn't listening. When I asked the students, "What do you want to do after high school?" they would answer, "I want to go to college." What I should have asked next is "Why?" But I didn't push or question because that was the answer I wanted to hear. But that was the time I should have pushed. What I would have heard was the students' desire to care for their parents, to be independent, to not rely on food stamps.

In truth, I was just like any refugee parent, hell-bent on all of my kids going to college. I was just like my own father, who didn't just insist on my going to college, he insisted that I get into one of the elite schools he had picked out for me. He even said that if I didn't I would have to stay and study at the University of Jordan (an embarrassment in my private-school circles). I was constantly taught to be the best and expect the best; anything less was unacceptable. College was my ticket out, and it was the ticket out for everyone — or so I believed.

Admitting to myself that college wasn't for each and every one of my students was an uncomfortable process. It makes other people uncomfortable when I talk about it. I've even been accused of giving up on them or lowering my standards. I get pushback from people who desperately want to believe that all things — that *anything* — is possible with hard work. But for our students, that is a dangerous, damaging narrative, one that ignores the challenges they have faced, their financial realities, and their own hopes and dreams.

I'm not supposed to say this: when a student enters middle school eight years behind, they are not going to regain all of that ground. We can narrow gaps. We can teach foundational skills. We can develop habits of mind, critical-thinking skills, and self-confidence. We can get them to a high school graduate level of proficiency. What we cannot do — no matter how hardworking or smart a child is or how committed their teachers are — is give our students back the time they have lost to war, famine, violence, and trauma. The educational capital and family financial health they might have had are not wholly retrievable. Pretending that if they really apply themselves they can get into and attend Harvard isn't just unrealistic, it's cruel.

Every single one of our students will get a college acceptance letter. We make sure of that. But instead of telling them that they can do the all but impossible (getting into and paying for and doing well at a top-tier school) or that a more accessible college degree will deliver the impossible (a guarantee that the debt they amass will be worth it in terms of career access and success) we need to redefine success, to expand our views of what it means to achieve it. I got a world-class education at Smith, but what really opened doors for me wasn't my degree; it was name recognition and a nationwide network. My degree told potential future employers, *This one is not a risk*. The small liberal arts college that Haben was accepted to, basically unknown outside of Georgia, couldn't offer those things to him, but he would have paid just as much to attend as my parents had paid for Smith. Our circumstances were different, our life experiences were different, so why should we expect our results to be exactly the same? It's time for us to admit that a one-size-fits-all version of success is only widening the gap between the haves and the have-nots. The systems and institutions that consistently fail students like mine don't suddenly go away once the students turn eighteen. Why do we keep pushing students into a system that is rigged against them?

Why can't we be just as enthusiastic about postsecondary pathways that don't include four-year colleges? Not as the plan B but as a respectable and impressive goal that isn't about further academic attainment? I believe we owe it to all students, not just refugee students, to answer that question with a resounding yes.

I have seen success without college, and I am not talking about Bill Gates or Mark Zuckerberg. The most memorable instance of this happened a decade before when I was hustling around the clock to open the café in Decatur. I had worked with carpenters, plumbers, and my favorite electrician, Wayne. Wayne was easily in his sixties and had done work for several restaurants in the area. He had a reputation for being honest, getting work done as promised — and not working weekends. I scheduled Wayne on the Friday before my Monday inspection, but the installation of my light fixtures ran way past schedule. Panicked, I asked him if he could stay for just a few more hours.

He looked at me like I was crazy. "I have to be home for dinner."

"Okay, what about tomorrow?"

"Don't work weekends. I go fishing on Saturdays. Out on my boat."

"Please?" I hated to beg. But if we didn't get the inspection done Monday, I'd have to push the opening back.

Wayne looked at me with pity. "Okay, I'll meet you here at 6 a.m. sharp tomorrow," he said. "But don't tell anyone."

He pulled up the next morning towing a twenty-foot fishing boat behind his truck. Here I was, bordering on broke, working twelve- to fourteen-hour days with my fancy college degree. And here was Wayne, doing his job the way he wanted to do it, enjoying his boat on a beautiful Saturday morning, making sure he had dinner with his family each night. Who was more successful? Would I be home for dinner every night with my family? Would I get to go fishing on my boat every weekend?

Whether or not Tesfay went to college should never have been about me or fundraising or anything else but Tesfay. But I was so focused on our goal—100 percent graduation rate, 100 percent college acceptance—that I refused to see other possibilities for him. I didn't listen. After fighting for so long to let my community speak for itself, I had imposed my own voice and values onto Tesfay.

No school should be judged strictly by the number of students who go on to college, especially if going to college represents a financial or personal burden for the student and especially if a college will not guarantee a better life for that student. Historically, college graduates have commanded a higher earning potential, but that doesn't mean any degree from any college is worth the high price of admission. Today, we are beginning to see a shift. Companies like Google are no longer requiring a college degree and are disrupting the education space by offering courses under its Google Career Certificates program at a fraction of the cost of a college degree. If we're distilling the value of education down to only earning potential, why aren't we pushing students to explore options in skilled trades so one day they can be their own boss like Wayne? Why don't we expand our definition of success to include vital professions like sonographers, X-ray technicians, and airplane mechanics, jobs that require an associate degree, and why don't we value them as much as we value someone with a bachelor's degree in economics or anthropology?

Funders and donors are hungry for secondary schools that go against the grain, that try new and innovative things — so long as these methods produce some version of that same tired story: rags to riches, refugee camp to Harvard, pulling yourself up by your own frayed bootstraps. Real innovation requires imagination. It requires flexibility. It requires us to talk together, to shut up, to listen, and above all, to question the status quo. It requires us to redefine success.

Not long after we started the school, we held a coat drive for our students. Bag after bag was dropped off at our door, some by familiar faces in the neighborhood, some by people we had never met. We were hoping for one hundred donations, and in the end, we received six hundred. Six hundred! We were blown away by the support for our community.

But then we began to go through the bags. We had been specific and asked for gently used or new jackets of a certain size, and we did get a few of those. But mostly we got junk. Other people's junk. Raggedy adult coats that would dwarf any one of our kids. Old unfolded clothes crudely jammed into trash bags. Canned goods past their expiration dates. Given the amount of time it took for us to sort through the bags — hours upon hours of valuable staff time — it would have been cheaper for us to purchase new coats for the kids.

One of our eighth graders, Bernice, stood behind a table, jackets stacked up based on size, everything else on the floor in piles beside her. Suddenly, in my peripheral vision, I saw Bernice get still. Then she got very quiet. I looked over at her as she plucked a pair of dishwater-colored men's underwear from the bag in front of her.

"They think we need . . . underwear?" she said. "That they wore?"

"Put it in the trash," I said.

My skin flushed with anger. It would be the last time we had a coat drive.

I think of encouraging all students to go to college no matter what — no matter if they can afford it, no matter if it will saddle them with profound debt, no matter if they want to or not — in the same way that I think about those bags of donations. As a false promise . . . full of shit. College can and has improved the lives of many, but it's hardly a sure bet. There's nothing wrong with not wanting to go to college. There's something very wrong with forcing everyone to go.

Today, I encourage our students who want to go to college to do so on their own terms with eyes wide open. That means understanding that higher education is rife with its own prejudiced and predatory practices — and that it's no magic bullet for prosperity, no guarantee of a high-paying job after graduation; and there's no guarantee that they will learn the skills they will need to establish the career they want.

It seems that social promotion doesn't end when high school does. According to Tom Lindsay, "A 50-plus-year nationwide study of the history of college grading finds that, in the early 1960s, an A grade was awarded in colleges nationwide 15 percent of the time. But today, an A is *the most common grade* given in college; the percentage of A grades has tripled, to 45 percent nationwide. Seventy-five percent of all grades awarded now are either A's and B's."

I have seen evidence of this in the job candidates who walk into my office. Over the years, I have seen how ill-prepared many college graduates are, with résumés full of errors and cover letters that are grammatically incorrect. I have sat across from MAs and PhDs in education, dumbfounded that I knew more than they did.

Too many billions of dollars in student loans have bought degrees, not skills. The current call to eliminate student debt doesn't go far enough; we must address the predatory practices at play in higher education.

It can be hard to spot them. Just like in the K–12 space, colleges enact seemingly progressive policies that make themselves look good but offer little in the way of change for students. For example, Ivy League schools like Harvard and Yale recently announced that they would provide full tuition remission for students whose families make less than $65,000 a year. But the students have to get in first — a formidable feat for kids who grow up in this income bracket. (The median family income for Harvard undergraduates is $168,800. More than 15 percent of kids who go to Harvard were raised in households making more than $630,000 per year.) Lower-middle-class kids who get into Harvard are outliers. This was a policy to make Harvard feel and look good, but it did little to address access. It's the same kind of tokenism we see at play in Ritz-Carlton's practice of bragging about hiring refugees but paying them just barely enough to get by. Harvard and the Ritz get great press, but the system never changes and the poor are kept in their place.

In this country, we love to tout the successful outlier. Michelle Obama grew up on the South Side of Chicago and went to Princeton . . . but also attended an academically elite magnet school. Her parents made great sacrifices for their children's education, including saving money by squeezing into a one-bedroom apartment so her mother could forego work and be hyperinvested in her kids' education instead. Sonia Sotomayor went from the housing projects in the South Bronx to the Supreme Court . . . but attended private Catholic schools. Bill Gates dropped out of college and became a billionaire . . . but needed his mother's connection with IBM to secure his first contract. Mark Zuckerberg also dropped out of college . . . and borrowed $100,000 from his dad to start Facebook. Why do we tell only half of these stories? The parts that suggest hard work is all it takes to be wildly successful? Why do we leave out the parts about engaged parents making profound sacrifices for their children's education and the seed money and the luck?

We rely on stories of outlier success because real change is hard

— and expensive. If colleges like Harvard and Yale were truly committed to equity, they would invest in K–12 education and use their extensive lobbying power to fight for high-quality education for all kids. They would establish innovative lab schools in the lowest-performing school districts, learning from those communities what needs to change in this country for all children to receive the kind of schooling that propels them into the Ivy League.

Today, our goal is not 100 percent college matriculation. It is to prevent the cycle of poverty from beginning. We all know how difficult it is to break that cycle, so it is essential that we ensure that it doesn't start. Over the years, we've developed a more practical approach to help students figure out what to do after high school. We weigh each opportunity and celebrate them equally. For some students, college is the right path. But for many others, it isn't. For those students, we make sure that they know all of their options — trade schools, apprenticeships, military service, career paths they can start on right away. Whatever it is, we want to help our kids begin to chart a path that will carry them to their own version of success. Maybe this means doing something they love. Maybe it's earning double or triple (or more) than what their parents earn. Maybe it means earning enough to take care of their parents.

I didn't have much of a choice about leaving Jordan. But I still feel guilt. In my culture, children have a responsibility to care for their parents as they age. There are no assisted-living facilities in the Middle East. As the firstborn, I would have been the designated caretaker, the errand runner, the appointment scheduler. No matter how much I recognize that I did not choose my current life, some part of me will always feel guilty about not meeting that obligation. For many years, I wasn't able to put that complicated feeling into words, then, as usual, the Fugees reminded me.

Haben was right. My job is not to beg; I am not beholden to an annual report or a grant application. My job is to make their lives better; I am beholden to them, my students.

I am complicit in a system that harms my students if I tell people only what they want to hear. We have to be authentic, bold, and proud. We have to tell our own stories. We have to dismantle the system.

Here are two stories I am extremely proud of.

"Can we talk?" The school's after-school coordinator, Hannah, hovered in my doorway.

"Sure," I answered, clicking send on an email I had finished writing.

Hannah conspicuously closed the door behind her. This couldn't be good. *Please don't quit,* I thought.

"I think you need to speak to Faven." When I didn't respond, Hannah continued, "Some of the after-school staff think she might be pregnant."

"Pregnant? Have you talked to her?"

"No, we think you should."

While I waited for Hannah to retrieve Faven, I breathed long and slow to steady myself. I knew this moment would come; it wasn't a matter of when but who.

Faven was Eritrean. She had long black hair and a high-wattage smile, but when she walked into my office, her face looked grim; that smile was nowhere in sight.

"How are you, Faven?" I asked.

"I am okay." She kept her eyes on the floor.

"Is there anything you need to talk about?"

"No. Maybe . . . I don't know." She touched her belly.

I let the silence linger. Waiting.

I left my chair and squatted next to the couch. "Are you pregnant?" *Please say no,* I thought. *Please say you've been eating too much American food.*

The tears began. "How did you know?"

I didn't tell Faven that at a school where exercise is part of the curriculum weight gain is uncommon.

"Does the father know?"

"Yes."

"Is he a Fugee?"

"No." Faven wiped her tears with the back of her sleeve. "Isaias has been telling me to speak to you for a few weeks. That you would know what to do." Isaias was another Eritrean student, almost like a big brother to Faven.

"To do?"

"About the baby."

I leaned back on my heels. "You're in a tough situation. But you have options. You can keep the baby even though you might have to raise it on your own. You could also give it up for adoption—"

"You mean, like, to someone else?"

"Yes."

"No. No way."

"Your other option is abortion."

"Kill it? My religion, my culture . . ."

"It's not kill—" I stopped myself. "You don't have to make any decisions right now. What does your mom think?"

Faven began sobbing, her small body rising and falling with each sharp breath.

"She doesn't know."

"She can't tell?" I asked.

"No," she said between heaves. "She's too . . . preoccupied." (Faven always liked to use her vocab words.)

"You have to tell her."

"She will be so disappointed. I can't."

"She loves you; it's going to be okay."

"My life is ruined! Everything is terrible."

"Nothing is ruined. Yes, this is rough. This is different from what you had imagined. But you will get through it. First, you need to tell your mom."

"Please, Coach. I can't." Faven put her head on my shoulder and cried even harder. Suddenly, she paused, lifted her tear-streaked face, and suggested the worst idea ever.

"You tell her."

When I sat down to talk to Faven's mother, I learned that she also had been a teen mother. Not only that, but *her* mother, Faven's grand-mother, had gotten pregnant at fourteen. It was one of the hardest conversations I've ever had — and I've had a lot of uncomfortable conversations.

Faven had the baby, a girl named Sesuna, in May. She wanted to take the next year, her junior year, off. I said absolutely not. I was sure that if she did she wouldn't come back. Instead, I cut a deal with her. I let her out of summer camp and the first semester of soc-cer practices. Faven knew that this was an unprecedented offer, so she accepted.

Together, we made it work. Faven's new reality meant that every day was a challenge, a puzzle that required flexibility and creativity to make sure the baby was cared for and Faven was getting her work done. It took some months for Faven's mother to come around, but her grandmother was unwavering in her support from the start, of-fering to babysit whenever she could. I watched Faven push through stress and exhaustion to remain a dedicated student — and a really good mom.

The summer before her senior year, she joined me and the rest of her class on a trip to Columbus to recruit our first sixth-grade class for the new campus. I'll never forget Faven, surrounded by her class-mates, gesticulating with her clipboard, telling everyone what they would be doing that day. Each of them hanging on her every word. I hadn't put her in charge — she just was. She expertly assigned tasks based on each of her classmates' strengths. And at the end of every day, she ran through the numbers with Nour and Dilva, saw who needed a follow-up the next day, which families needed an extra nudge. She assigned a leader for each visit.

She also did the impossible — she got Thamein and Adam to chop onions, tomatoes, and garlic when she made us a delicious meal. She showed what is possible when strong women are allowed to lead.

Faven graduated on time; her daughter even walked up on stage in the middle of Faven's speech! She had been accepted to college like everyone else in her class, but as her classmates made plans for fall semester at college or for starting apprenticeships, she kept changing her mind. She talked about becoming a plumber or a daycare worker. I waited to see what would happen.

Knowing when to step back, when to reach out, when to have a heavy hand — these are skills that I continue to refine.

Faven moved to Denver to be with the baby's father but came back to Georgia after just a few months. Emily and I moved to Columbus. All the while, we remained in contact via text; I tried to tread lightly. To let Faven find her way, to let her know I was here to help if she needed me to.

One day she texted to ask about the name of the Montessori school our girls had attended in Atlanta.

"Are you looking for a job?" I asked. I knew Faven had been interested in working with kids.

"No, for Sesuna, I am looking at different options for her."

I hesitated. I wondered if Faven knew about the tuition.

Faven read my mind. "I have a job, Coach. A good job."

"You do? Where?"

"At the chicken factory."

My heart dropped. If there was one thing I wanted for all of our kids, it was a life better than their parents had, one that didn't include working at the poultry plants where so many of our families spent long, hard days.

I gave myself a little pep talk (don't react, don't judge, don't lose your temper) and called Faven by phone.

"Don't worry, Coach!" Faven said. "I know you are flipping out, but it's good."

"I am not flipping out!" I said. "Okay, maybe a little. Just tell me about it."

"Well, you were right. I needed my high school diploma."

I waited.

"I am a manager, a supervisor!"

"But you've only been there a few months."

"I know how to read English and do math, so I supervise and manage the formulas for marinating chicken." I began to relax as Faven excitedly told me all about her new job. She bragged that her boss had plans to train her in a number of different departments. She was now overseeing the group her mother worked in. She was making eighteen dollars an hour, enough to support her family of two.

Our phone call had taken place as I drove home from school. As I pulled the car in front of the house, I leaned my head back against the car seat and let a few tears fall. Faven was happy. I was happy.

When I walked in the front door, my daughters ran to greet me. I picked them up and kissed their heads.

"Are you okay?" Emily asked, leaning in the doorway to the kitchen. She could tell my eyes were red.

"More than okay," I said. "Faven is working at the chicken factory. It's so good."

For a minute, I think Emily was sure that I had finally, completely lost it.

"It's so good," I said to my girls, who knew and adored Faven. I wanted the same thing for them that I wanted for her — to find satisfying work, to have a more fulfilling life than their parents had, and to be self-sufficient and secure. And now they had one more role model to show them how it's done.

After eighth grade at Fugees Academy, Abdullahi had graduated from his high school four years later with a 4.3 GPA. His SAT scores were 640 — combined. Terrible. His school's social promotion and grade inflation were made all too clear. When Abdullahi asked me for advice about college, I wasn't sure what to tell him.

I started researching career paths that didn't require a four-year degree. I looked for industries that reported current labor shortages and read about what skills employers would be looking for in five to ten years. I stumbled upon an article about air traffic controllers — and read that in the coming years a wave of retirements would mean lots of lucrative job openings. I was shocked to learn that salaries for air traffic controllers were often in the six figures and that to be one you needed only an associate degree. It just so happened that Georgia has the only public aviation program in the country.

Abdullahi was excited by the possibility. We looked over the website together and visited the school. I was relieved by the price — and that Abdullahi would be required to take a semester of remediation offered by the college. In a perfect world, colleges wouldn't need to offer remedial courses because high schools would do their jobs. But what mattered to me most now was Abdullahi's success.

For a while, that looked like a sure thing. Until Abdullahi's father got cancer. After completing his associate degree, Abdullahi moved back to Clarkston to take care of his parents and took the first job he could find — working as a parking valet. When he could, he volunteered at the Fugees Academy as a tutor and coach. One year turned into two. Abdullahi was still parking cars. I tried to tread lightly, to let him find his way. Mostly, I did very well at this. Until I didn't.

One day I took him out to lunch at a quiet Nepalese restaurant close to the school.

"Are you going to valet for the rest of your life?"

"No, but right now I have to. It's good money and I can pay for the cancer treatments."

"But you worked your butt off to get your degree. What is stopping you from getting the job?"

Abdullahi shook his head. "I can't; I have to pay for the treatments."

I got quiet. "You will always have an excuse not to do this. Something will always come up that you will need to fix or take care of. But you can take better care of others if you are happy and take care of yourself first. That doesn't mean not paying for the treatments or supporting your family. But a better job will help you take better care of them."

Abdullahi's eyes filled with tears. "The other day my mom asked, 'You get a degree to fix airplanes and you are parking cars?' I know I've disappointed you and them."

"So why aren't you fixing airplanes? You told me you loved it."

"The mechanic's-license test. It costs fifteen hundred dollars. But the rent and the cancer —"

"Why didn't you say something?"

"I couldn't, Coach. I know you. You've done enough."

I moved the half-empty plate aside and put my hands on the table.

"We are going back to the office right now. It's a loan, okay? You have a year to pay it off. I don't have fifteen hundred dollars to lose. But it's zero percent interest because I am also Muslim," I joked. At this, Abdullahi smiled.

"One year?"

"One year."

Abdullahi took his test and passed. He paid off his loan within a year. Even though Abdullahi lived near the largest airport in the South, there weren't any jobs in Atlanta, so he applied for and got a job with American Airlines outside of Cincinnati. He sent most of his first months' paychecks back home to his parents.

Abdullahi's father succumbed to the cancer not long after the move. When he texted to tell me, Abdullahi wrote, "I am glad he got to see me be an airplane mechanic and be successful."

"Me, too," I wrote back.

A few months later, Abdullahi called to tell me that he was sending me an email; he waited as I opened it and clicked on the attached link. It was the log-in to his American Airlines profile. He had listed me as his mother, so I could receive the discount the airline offered to family members.

"I am not your mother," I said.

"I know, Coach, but she doesn't fly, and they don't have a 'coach' category."

Not long ago, I was pleasantly surprised to get a text from Abdullahi. It was a picture of a beautiful redbrick house with a two-car garage and big front porch. It looked familiar to me, but I couldn't place it.

"What is this?" I wrote.

Abdullahi wrote back. "It's a house, Coach."

"I know it's a house, but why are you sending it to me?"

"I bought it for my mom."

"You bought a house for your mom?"

"Yes, it's right by your old house in Clarkston."

For a few seconds, I stared at the photo in disbelief. Then I called Abdullahi so he could tell me all about it.

AN OPPORTUNITY
LIKE NO OTHER

O N MARCH 13, 2020, WE CLOSED OUR SCHOOLS. AT first, like everyone else, we assumed that the coronavirus crisis would last a couple of weeks, that by mid-April things would be back to normal.

Of course, two weeks turned into the rest of the school year. We canceled prom, we canceled graduation, our soccer season was suspended. The following August, we made the wrenching decision to continue remote learning even though we knew our students were anxious and lonely and falling behind in their work. But the only thing more important than their education was their safety and the safety of their families, so we stayed closed.

That fall, a teenager in our neighborhood named Jay came to the front door. He was looking to make some extra money and wanted to know if he could rake our leaves. I told him he could rake our yard, then I asked why he wasn't in school.

"Are you a principal?" Jay asked wearily.

"Kinda," I said. "Why?"

"I can just tell."

"So why aren't you in school?"

"It's online. I can't learn like that and no one even makes sure I'm there. It's easier to go out and earn some money."

Jay was like the thousands of kids across the country who were "disappearing" or not showing up to school during COVID. (When our students stopped showing up to online classes, coaches drove over to their houses and knocked on doors.)

A few weeks later, Jay came by selling cookies.

"How much?" I said, my hand on my wallet.

"One dollar."

"That's too much—I can get a cookie for seventy-five cents at Panera."

"Okay, fifty cents," Jay countered.

"You should have told me that yours are better than Panera's, that's why they're a dollar." (Sometimes the entrepreneur in me won't leave well enough alone.)

"Oh. Yeah."

"That's okay—go try it on Ken," I said, pointing across the street. "I'll take a dozen."

"A dozen?" I could tell by Jay's face that the word was foreign to him.

"Twelve."

At this, Jay pulled up the calculator on his phone.

"Jay, what math class are you in?"

"I'm in tenth grade—so I'm in geometry."

I thought about Jay for days after that exchange. Raking leaves while he should have been in school, reliant on a calculator for the most basic math equations. Jay goes to the school in our neighborhood, the one we won't send our kids to. Just like my parents didn't send me to the government schools in Jordan. The cycle spins on.

The pandemic brought us all to our knees. It also forced us to look at—to stare at for months on end—every flaw and inequality in our shared systems, particularly our schools. We were surprised, it seemed, that without a school cafeteria millions of children didn't eat. We were dumbfounded that families had to park their car in the McDonald's parking lot to access the internet. Parents were horrified as leaders — everyone from their governors to their superintendents — continued to punt decisions about when and how to reopen for fear of sinking their political careers; they wondered why there was enough will and ingenuity to host an NBA tournament but not to educate their kids. The coronavirus didn't create these conditions so much as it made us hold still and look long and hard into the mirror.

By January of the new year, Fugees schools couldn't wait anymore. We knew we needed to reopen. So we rallied the troops — parents, teachers, school leaders — and we figured out a way to get the Fugees back in the classroom. In the end, it was easier than I thought it would be. We had spent so many years earning the faith of our families that when we needed their trust they didn't hesitate. They knew we would take care of their children no matter what.

This flexibility, the capacity to cater to the needs of our specific community, is what undergirds our school at all times, not just during a crisis, and it's something that most public schools lack. Fugees Academy would not exist without school choice. I'm not saying charter and private schools are *the* answer to all our problems. Just like there are terrible public schools, there are charter schools that should be shut down and private schools I wouldn't set foot in. Bad schools are everywhere; good schools are not.

We have to move away from the destructive idea that in order for our education system to be fair and equal classrooms and curriculums need to be identical. True equity would mean accommodating the needs of every child regardless of their background, ability, or learning style.

The reason charter schools were established in the first place was to serve as innovation incubators where teachers and administrators could experiment with new ideas that might then be applied in the larger district — the same way a fast-food company tries out new menus in a test market. Even Albert Shanker, the head of the country's second-largest teachers' union, endorsed the idea of charter schools in 1988, arguing that the solutions identified in charter schools would build a stronger, more sustainable public education system.

In many ways, the Fugees Academy has been an innovation incubator. We now have a proven model. But my vision is not to open a Fugees Academy in every state or resettlement community.

Had the pandemic never happened, right now our team would likely be getting ready to launch a new school in St. Louis or Indianapolis. But those months of deep self-reflection germinated the seed of an idea that had been growing for years, one that was fed by the recurrent thought that so many of us had during the endless solitary months of lockdown: *we cannot go back to normal.* For the country as a whole, that means, for instance, making sure that all kids have access to high-speed internet. For us, that means shifting our focus. Opening more schools isn't going to solve the problem. It would make the lives of our students better, of course. But what about other refugee kids all over America? What about the teachers who aren't given the training or resources to teach them? What about the policies that impede refugee education?

And so I've begun work that I hope will put the Fugees Family out of business. It's an initiative we're calling Teranga, the Senegalese word for community, and it focuses on scaling our model at newcomer programs like the kind Jean Claude attended. We're taking everything we've learned in fifteen years and spreading it far and wide. Soon, when refugee children arrive at the newcomer center in their city, they won't simply memorize a few English phrases and learn about American holidays. Instead, they will enroll in a curriculum that emphasizes holistic English acquisition, a trauma-informed approach to schooling, and integrated athletics for all during year-round programming.

Our current academies will act as hubs for disseminating the training teachers need to deliver this curriculum by having educators participate in online and onsite Fugees-model training. In this training, teachers will hone their ability to serve refugee students, English-language learners, and displaced youth more effectively. These trainings will fill a void; there aren't any like them in the nation.

At the same time, Teranga will be working with partner organizations to advocate for policy change on education issues at the local, state, and federal levels, including lobbying for firm requirements for school districts in relation to this student population, such as increasing the time arriving students spend at newcomer schools and raising the mandatory graduation age.

If this seems like a lot of effort for a niche population, consider that by 2025 a quarter of students in American public schools will be English-language learners. America is changing and our education system must too. We cannot continue to tweak a little and hope it gets better.

I would never be able to do this kind of work in Jordan. I also wouldn't be able to criticize a government that fails its citizens (I would be locked up for that). It is an incredible privilege and an expression of patriotism to be able to say this out loud: our system is broken and we need to fix it.

Like most immigrants, I fell in love with America through television. As a little girl in Jordan, I marveled at the Americans I saw on TV: the smart and formidable Mrs. Huxtable and the suburban family that protected an illegal alien named E.T. Only in America could four old ladies share their golden years (and their sexual exploits) in a handsome Miami home; only in America could a buxom woman kidnap her boss and commandeer the company. In my mind, the United States was a place where police officers defended their communities (*CHiPs*), ingenuity was boundless (*Knight Rider*), and the daughter of a poor teen mom could win three Olympic gold medals (Jackie Joyner-Kersee).

America was the land of equality, inclusion, and innovation. Light-years ahead of the rest of us. I'll never forget when my uncle Ghassan gifted me with an Apple IIe. He told me that the computer had been built in a garage in America. There was so much greatness in America that even the garages were brimming with it.

In America, I thought, my grandparents would never have had to flee their home to run from their own government. My mother would not have been bullied; she would have gone on to college and had her own career. In America, I wouldn't have to hide who I really was.

In a lot of ways, the America I found was a surprise, a disappointment. Black women, it turned out, weren't so equal. The poor were othered and ostracized. Gay people endured discrimination, hate crimes, and sometimes, just like in my country, even death. Refugee kids like the ones I saw in that camp languished here just like they did there.

America wasn't the land I had been imagining all my life. It wasn't the jackpot that so many refugee families fantasized about during years of upheaval. Maybe I created Fugees Academy because I so desperately wanted what we believed to be true. I wanted to live in *that* America, the country that finds solutions, that doesn't settle for second or third or thirty-sixth.

I owe my life to this nation, and in many ways, that's what I have given it.

After all, America is still the place — the *only* place — where a gay Muslim from the Middle East could marry a Jewish woman from the Midwest, have three beautiful children, and open not one but two schools for refugees from every hungry and ravaged country on Earth. It is the place where those refugee kids can bloom and thrive, settle ancient geopolitical disputes simply by pulling out a chair at the lunch table. These stories—our stories—show us what is still possible in this country that we love so much. I wish I could tell my grandmother these stories. I wish she could see my students walk across the stage and accept their diplomas; I wish she could see the pride and relief in their parents' eyes.

I wish, too, that I could talk to her when I feel frustrated or hopeless, to lament how impossible it can seem when so many people are suffering and so many others are indifferent.

But I know what she would say: that there is no time for despair or self-congratulation. No time to stand still. *Shoo baidein, habibti?* she would ask. And now I ask you, too.

What next?

AFTERWORD

Since *Learning America* went to press in 2022, we have made important strides toward accomplishing our vision for Teranga Academy: to change American education by spreading far and wide everything we've learned through the Fugees model in the past twenty years. In December 2022, we were awarded a federal Education Innovation and Research grant, a significant milestone that allows us to rigorously test and build a solid research foundation to back up our strategies and to expand the reach of our model to school districts across the country.

Two students, Zuri and Tomas, from our first public school district partnership in Bowling Green, Kentucky, embody everything we aim to achieve.

Zuri's journey through the American education system had not been easy. She was born in Tanzania and came to the United States when she was eleven years old. She was enrolled in the Bowling Green Independent School District in Kentucky for fifth and sixth grades, where she struggled to fit in. At the junior high, she faced bullying, had difficulty making friends, and was often tardy or absent.

Then came Teranga, and everything shifted. Over the next two years, Zuri missed just one day of school. She would often talk about how Teranga felt like a family to her. I'll never forget when she said, "I want to show people that the old Zuri is gone. The new Zuri believes in herself." Her transformation was remarkable: she went from feeling lost to dreaming about becoming a doctor or returning to Teranga to teach the next generation.

Her academic growth matched this newfound confidence. After only one year at Teranga, her English proficiency score soared and after two years she was able to move on from multilingual-learner services entirely. In the spring of her second year at Teranga, she took the state assessment, scoring distinguished in reading and proficient in math and writing. But it wasn't just about the scores. She was reading independently, creating incredible artwork, and singing at the top of her lungs, brimming with pride and belief in herself. Zuri's story reminds me that the problem is never the students who are failing, it's the system that's failing them.

Tomas's path was different but his story is equally powerful. He started at Teranga under difficult circumstances, missing twenty-six days in his first semester. When we sat down with him to talk, we learned that his living situation was challenging. He had come to the US alone, expecting to live with his sponsor, an uncle. But his uncle had moved out of state, abandoning Tomas to live with two young men he barely knew. He was struggling to pay his share of the rent and expenses, all while trying to attend school. After we strategized with Tomas on balancing school and work, his attendance improved, and he missed only three days of school in the remainder of the term.

In the spring of his first year at Teranga, Tomas shared his immigration portfolio with Kristi Costellow, the principal of Teranga Academy in Bowling Green. We discovered that Tomas was eligible for a Special Immigrant Juvenile (SIJ) visa. We called in a favor with an immigration attorney and within a year Tomas had his visa and was on the path to citizenship. I'll always remember telling Kristi that Tomas had a potential pathway forward. Her response was, "If you do this for him, you'll have to do it for all the other kids who are eligible." She was right. As her mentor and coach for the previous three years I had seen Kristi grow into a compassionate leader, dedicated to pushing herself and her team to do the best for every student and family. I had guided her, and now she was challenging me to step up and do more. At that moment, Kristi pushed me to see a larger vision. It reminded me of an old adage: "The true measure of a teacher is when the student surpasses the master."

Now, at Teranga Academy, we ensure that every student who qualifies for the SIJ visa has the same opportunity for a path to citizenship. We continue to innovate and have created a robust work program that allows older students like Tomas to earn money while working toward a high school diploma.

The data year after year continues to surpass everyone's expectations. The students' average growth in reading and math has been more than 250 percent. Kristi leads her team in implementing the model, driving it forward, pushing for greater impact and equity. Through our partnership, we support Kristi and her incredible team as they transform the academic achievement of and educational experience for their multilingual learners.

Teranga Academy is actively searching for new partners across the United States who are prepared to embark on the multiyear, transformative experience of establishing a vibrant newcomer program within their district or network. A strong leader who believes in the vision is key to success of the program. From day one, superintendent Gary Fields was that leader for Bowling Green, saying, "We can do better for our multilingual population." Gary believed in the Fugees model and worked tirelessly to ensure that it was implemented with fidelity. His legacy will be that he changed the trajectory for refugee and immigrant students, moving mountains to make sure they had what they needed to thrive. It's because of leaders like Gary and educators like Kristi that our vision continues to grow, touching more lives and transforming more communities across the country.

ACKNOWLEDGMENTS

"Write a book," they said. But I didn't have anything to share, had accomplished nothing worth writing about. I wasn't good at it; I couldn't do it. But then the puzzle pieces came together and I started to write, to tell my own story as Ishmael Beah, the Sierra Leonean writer, had encouraged me to do years ago.

Laurene Powell Jobs, you upended the puzzle box and showed me all of the beautiful pieces. Without your unending support and encouragement, this story would have remained untold. Thank you for encouraging me to put words on paper, for believing in me and the power of the voices that needed to be heard.

To my agent, Todd Shuster, and the team at Aevitas, your commitment to this book and the patience and optimism you so generously gave throughout the entire process made it a reality.

Lauren Sharp, your superb matchmaking skills set me up with the best collaborator one could ever wish for. Ashley Stimpson, your remarkable ability to guide, wordsmith, and organize chaotic thoughts all while having an incredible sense of humor, humility, and compassion made this book what it is. Jeff, Dianne, and Nigel, thank you for sharing this extraordinary human with me this year.

All good coaches bring out the best in their players. Deanne Urmy, you saw this book before I did. Your tough love kept pushing me to make everything better. Thank you for never settling for good enough.

David Hough, you had me at "wicket"; thank you for your smart and meticulous edits. And thank you to Kerry Rubenstein and Davide Bonazzi for partnering to produce the beautiful book cover; it was well worth the wait.

Kevin Jennings, Mona Sinha, David Buchalter, Gary Smith, Abby Schumwinger, and Kathy Kennedy, thank you for being real, for giving honest feedback in early drafts, and for your unwavering mentorship and guidance this past year.

Debbe Sugrue, thank you for your unwavering friendship, generosity, and support; you insist on seeing the best in me, in the Fugees, and in my family, and we are all better for it.

Writing a book during a pandemic might make sense, but writing a book while operating two schools during a pandemic is not necessarily the best idea.

To my deeply dedicated board of directors, your tireless work behind the scenes is what allows the ship to keep sailing. Shola Oni, Eason Jordan, David Williams, Asha Rangaraj, Katie Hammer, Rachel Farren, Carl Fowler, Mohamed Soltan, Waleed Nassar, Diana Fleming, Marni Mohr, Sara Beth Watson, Ed Lindsey, Ron Abercrombie, Hawa Mohammed, and Zahra Hussein, thank you for sharing and supporting the vision of the Fugees. Your generous gifts of time and expertise are greatly appreciated.

Fugees staff and teachers: I feel so lucky to work with you. You are the ones making it all happen. This past year has tested everyone in working in education. You remained strong and relentless, and went the extra mile each and every single day for our community. You are the only team that could have gotten us through this past year.

And to all of the Fugees I have been privileged to coach: You have touched and changed my life in ways you will never understand.

Your resilience gave me hope and faith in the power of the human spirit. You've given me reason to believe that anything is possible.

Amanda Adelman, Dee-Ann Durbin, Sheherezade Essack, Allison Rohe, Chelsea Wilkerson, and Misty Wyman, you are my Smith sisters. You can always tell who your true friends are when you hit rock bottom. Thank you for being my family and piecing me back together over and over again. All with compassion, kindness, and a sick sense of humor.

Mama, this book has a lot of stories about strong women, but I left out the story of the strongest woman I know because I could not do it justice. Baba, you have been a voice of reason in this chaotic world. You have both supported me and pushed me to be my best. In spite of the bumpy road we've taken to get here, I know your love knows no bounds.

Among the many gifts Mama and Baba gave me were Ali, Said, and Inam. Irreplaceable and always annoying. Even though we share the same parents, you all know that I am the smart one.

Noura Alnashar, my Syrian sister, for bringing the smells, tastes, and laughter of Syria back into my life.

Leila, Zeina, and Yazan, our morning dance parties and your constant "Aren't you finished with your book yet?" were just the motivation I needed to complete a book during a pandemic. I am so sorry that it doesn't have any pictures or farts. Jessi, Meg, Mark, and Arlyn, thank you for helping care for the mischievous munchkins; it definitely took a village. Carol and David, Nancy and David, the love and support from you has been immeasurable.

And the final puzzle piece, the one who made the separate whole — Emily. Rohi. Albi. I promise you I'll hang up the writer's hat you gave me for at least a little while once this goes to press. It's been a roller coaster of a year. Thank you for believing in me, for being my biggest cheerleader, and for holding everything together while I was writing. Without you, this wouldn't have been possible.

APPENDIX I

SEEKING ASYLUM

U.S. Immigration & Naturalization Service
Asylum Office
1200 Wall Street West, 4th Floor
Lyndhurst, New Jersey 07071

September 10, 1998

Ms. Luma H MUFLEH
70 Jamaica Way, #2
Jamaica Plain, MA 02130

Re: A73 651 950 Luma H. MUFLEH

<u>**Asylum Approval**</u>

Dear Ms. MUFLEH:

This letter refers to your request for asylum in the United States filed on Form I-589. This office previously issued you a letter to notify you that your request for asylum had been recommended for approval, pending the results of the mandatory, confidential investigation of your identity and background.

It has been determined that you are eligible for asylum in the United States. Attached please find a completed Form I-94, Arrival Departure Record, indicating that you have been granted asylum status in the United States pursuant to §208(a) of the Immigration and Nationality Act (INA) as of September 10, 1998. You have been granted asylum in the United States for an indefinite period. This grant of asylum includes your dependents listed above who are present in the United States, were included in your asylum application, and for whom you have established a qualifying relationship by a preponderance of evidence.

In order to request derivative asylum status for any spouse or child who was not included in your asylum request, you must submit a Form I-730, Refugee and Asylee Relative Petition, to the Immigration and Naturalization Service (INS).

You are eligible for employment authorization for as long as you remain in asylum status. Your dependents listed above are also eligible for employment authorization, so long as they retain derivative asylum status. However, you must apply for and obtain an Employment Authorization Document (EAD) as evidence of your eligibility to work in the United States. To obtain an EAD, you must submit to the INS a Form I-765, Application for Employment Authorization. We suggest that you include a copy of this letter when applying for work authorization as an asylee.

If you plan to depart the United States, you must obtain permission to return to the United States before you leave the country. If you do not obtain permission, you may be unable to reenter the United States, or you may be placed in proceedings where you will be required to establish your asylum status. You may apply for a Refugee Travel Document on a Form I-131, Application for Travel Document.

Asylum status does not give you the right to remain permanently in the United States. Asylum status may be terminated if you no longer have a well-founded fear of persecution because of a fundamental change in circumstances, you have obtained protection from another country, or you have committed certain crimes or engaged in other activity that makes you ineligible to retain asylum status in the United States. See INA §208(c)(2) and 8 C.F.R. §208.22(a).

You may apply for lawful permanent resident status under §209(b) of the Immigration and Nationality Act after you have been physically present in the United States for a period of one year after the date you were granted asylum status. To apply for lawful permanent residence, you must submit to the INS a Form I-485, Application to Register Permanent Residence or Adjust Status.

You must notify the INS of any change of address within ten days of any such change. You may obtain a Form AR-11 at your nearest post office or INS office to comply with this requirement.

You may obtain any of the forms noted above at an INS District Office or INS Forms Center. Instructions with or on the forms explain how to complete the forms, what documents to attach and where to send the completed forms.

Sincerely,

Susan Dibbins
Director
Newark Asylum Office

Enclosure: I-94

cc: Richard L. Landoli, Esq.
Landoli and Associates
36 Melrose Street
Boston, MA 02116

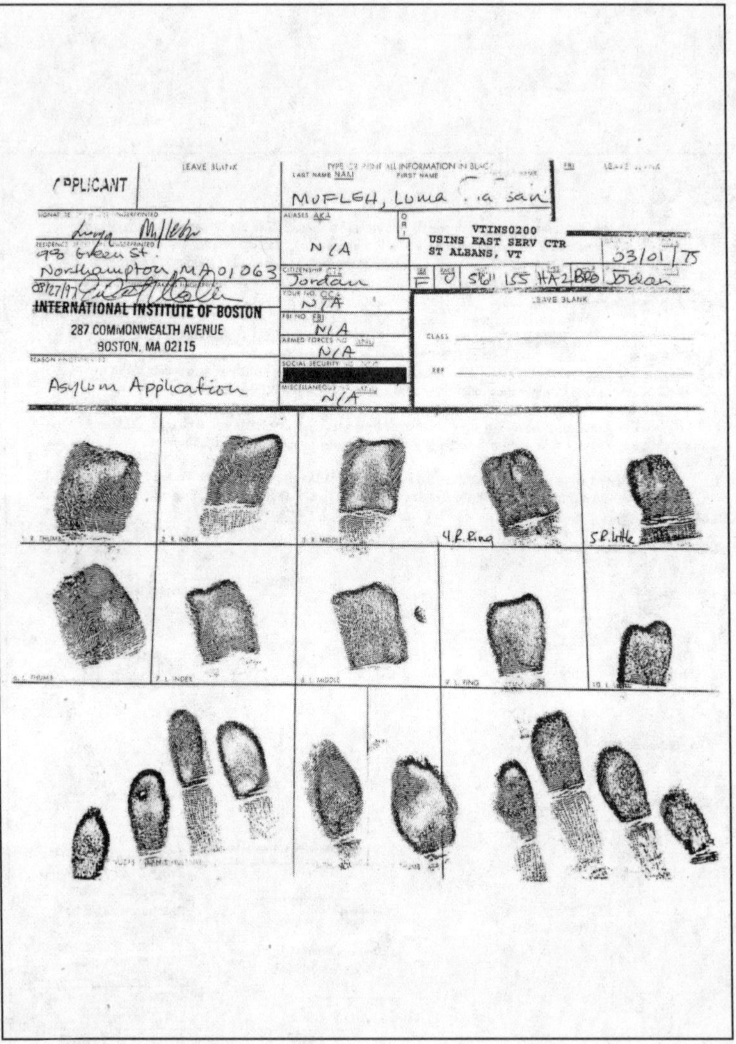

INTERNATIONAL GAY AND LESBIAN HUMAN RIGHTS COMMISSION ASYLUM PROJECT

US ASYLUM FACT SHEET

Definition of a Refugee: an individual who is unable or unwilling to return to his/her country because of persecution or a well-founded fear of persecution on account of race, religion, nationality, membership in a particular social group or political opinion (8 USC §1101 (a) (42) (A) (1982)).

Important Cases

Matter of Toboso-Alfonso [A23-220-644] Int. Dec. 3222 (BIA 1990)

Immigration Judge Robert Brown granted Fidel Armando Toboso-Alfonso's application for withholding of deportation to Cuba on February 3, 1986. Judge Brown concluded that Toboso was a member of a particular social group (homosexuals) who feared persecution by the Cuban Government. On March 12, 1990 the Board of Immigration Appeals upheld the decision. On June 16, 1994 Attorney General Reno ordered this decision to be a legal precedent.

Matter of Tenorio [A72-093-558] (IJ 1993)

Immigration Judge Philip Leadbetter ruled on July 26, 1993 that Marcelo Tenorio, a Brazilian gay man, was eligible for asylum because of his well founded fear of persecution on account of his membership in a particular social group. The ruling is currently under appeal by the INS before the Board of Immigration Appeals.

Matter of Pitcherskaia [A72-143-932] (BIA 1995)

In a divided panel decision, the BIA ruled in November 1995 that a Russian lesbian who had been constantly arrested by the police, threatened with psychiatric institutionalization to change her sexual orientation and was expelled from school and lost jobs, failed to demonstrate a well-founded fear of persecution. The BIA held that each of her experiences did not rise to the level of persecution and the Russia government only intended to "cure" her of her sexual orientation rather than "punish" her. BIA Chairperson Schmidt dissented, and would have granted asylum based on the psychiatric persecution. A petition for review by the Ninth Circuit is pending. The American Civil Liberties Union, the American Immigration Lawyers Association, Amnesty International USA, Human Rights Watch, the International Human Rights Law Group, the Lawyers Committee for Civil Rights, the Lawyers Committee for Human Rights, the National Center for Lesbian Rights, the National Immigration Project of the National Lawyers' Guild and IGLHRC have filed amici briefs in support of Pitcherskaia.

Asylum Cases Granted

Mar 18, 1994.......... G/Mexico	Sep 13, 1995............L/Ethiopia	May 10, 1996 ....G/Russia
Aug 31, 1994........ G/Pakistan	Oct 3, 1995..............G/Pakistan	May 20, 1996...........G/Mexico
Oct 18, 1994 .... G/Turkey	Oct 18, 1995.............L/Iran	May 29, 1996............L/Russia
Nov 17, 1994 .... G/Colombia	Oct 31, 1995............H/Togo-Ivory Cst	Jun 5, 1996............G(2)/Russia
Feb 7, 1995............ G/Nicaragua	Nov 14, 1995...........G/El Salvador	Jun 23, 1996............GH/El Salvador
Feb 23, 1995.......... G/Venezuela	Jan 5, 1996..............G/Guatemala	Jun 25, 1996............iG/China
Mar 10, 1995.......... G/Singapore	Jan 17, 1996 ....G/Colombia	Jun 28, 1996............G/El Salvador
Mar 31, 1995.......... G/Eritrea	Feb 15, 1996............G/Romania	Jul 5, 1996............G/Romania
Apr 5, 1995............ G/Iran	Feb 20, 1996............G/Brazil	Jul 23, 1996............G/Colombia
Apr 18, 1995........... G/Brazil	Feb 26, 1996............GH/Colombia	Jul 23, 1996............G/Yemen
Apr 19, 1995........... G/Honduras	Mar 11, 1996............G/Jordan	Jul 26, 1996............GH/Brazil
May 30, 1995........... G/Lebanon	Mar 13, 1996............L/Guatemala	Aug 6, 1996............H/Brazil
Jun 16, 1995 .... GH/Brazil	Mar 19, 1996............G/Venezuela	Aug 13, 1996............GH/Brazil
Jul 5, 1995............ TF/Colombia	Mar 29, 1996............G/Iran	Aug 27, 1996............G/Iran
Jul 18, 1995............ G/Iran	Apr 2, 1996 ....G/El Salvador	Sep 3, 1996............G/Pakistan
Jul 24, 1995........... G/Mexico	Apr 2, 1996 ....G/Peru	Sep 10, 1996............G/Mauritania
Aug 4, 1995............ L/Colombia	Apr 11, 1996............G/Pakistan	Sep 11, 1996............G/Pakistan
Aug 14, 1995 .... G/Albania	Apr 15, 1996............G/Russia	
Sep 1, 1995............ G/Nicaragua	Apr 22, 1996............GH/Chile	
Sep 6, 1995............ G/Eritrea	Apr 29, 1996............G/Pakistan	

Codes

H (person with HIV/AIDS), G (gay man), L (lesbian), B (bisexual)
TF (male-to-female transgender), TM (female-to-male transgender), i imputed ground

[IGLHRC§961002]

Asylum Project
International Gay and Lesbian Human Rights Commission
1360 Mission Street, Suite 200 San Francisco, CA 94103 USA
Tel +1 415 255 8680 Fax + 1 255 8662
E-mail: (Asylum Project) asylum@iglhrc.org, (IGLHRC) iglhrc@iglhrc.org
http://www.iglhrc.org

APPENDIX II

REFUGEE RESETTLEMENT

TOP REFUGEE RESETTLEMENT HUBS IN THE U.S. (CITIES) 2015–2019 AVERAGES

CITY	RANKING PER CAPITA	# OF REFUGEES PER 10,000 RESIDENTS
Clarkston, GA	1	170
Lancaster, PA	2	59.4
Bowling Green, KY	3	56.3
West Springfield, MA	4	56.0
Syracuse, NY	5	50.4
Utica, NY	6	48.8
Troy, MI	7	47.6
Erie, PA	8	44.6
New Bern, NC	9	43.8
Twin Falls, ID	10	42.2

CITY	RANKING PER # OF RESETTLED REFUGEES	# OF REFUGEES RESETTLED PER YEAR
Houston, TX	1	1,295
San Diego, CA	2	1,251
Dallas, TX	3	1,138
Buffalo, NY	4	1,035
Chicago, IL	5	1,030
Columbus, OH	6	983
Indianapolis, IN	7	962
Phoenix, AZ	8	927
Louisville, KY	9	905
Portland, OR	10	793

(from American Public Media Research Lab)

TOP TEN ORIGINS OF REFUGEE ARRIVALS TO THE UNITED STATES, FY 2010, FY 2020, AND FY 2010-20

FY 2010			FY 2020
ORIGIN	NUMBER	PERCENT	ORIGIN
Iraq	18,016	24.6	Dem. Rep. Congo
Myanmar	16,693	22.8	Myanmar
Bhutan	12,363	16.9	Ukraine
Somalia	4,884	6.7	Afghanistan
Cuba	4,818	6.6	Iraq
Iran	3,543	4.8	Syria
Dem. Rep. Congo	3,174	4.3	Eritrea
Eritrea	2,570	3.5	El Salvador
Palestine	1,053	1.4	Moldova
Vietnam	891	1.2	Sudan
All other countries, including unknown	5,306	7.2	All other countries, including unknown
Total	73,311	100.0	Total

Source: MPI analysis of the State Department's Worldwide Refugee Admissions Processing System data.

	NUMBER	PERCENT	FY 2010–2020 TOTAL		
			ORIGIN	NUMBER	PERCENT
	2,868	24.3	Myanmar	125,137	20.8
	2,115	17.9	Iraq	109,412	18.2
	,927	16.3	Bhutan	77,409	12.9
	504	5.1	Dem. Rep. Congo	70,447	11.7
	537	4.5	Somalia	54,211	9.0
	481	4.1	Iran	22,573	3.8
	475	4.0	Syria	22,163	3.7
	365	3.1	Cuba	20,020	3.3
	364	3.1	Ukraine	19,237	3.2
	254	2.1	Eritrea	18,223	3.0
	,824	15.4	All other countries, including unknown	62,028	10.3
	1,814	100.0	Total	600,860	100.0

ANNUAL REFUGEE RESETTLEMENT CEILING AND NUMBER OF REFUGEES ADMITTED TO THE UNITED STATES, FY 1980–2021

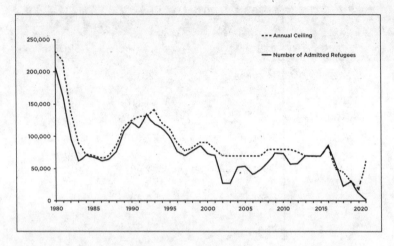

Notes: Data on admitted refugees for FY 2021 run through April 30, 2021; the FY 2017 refugee ceiling was originally 110,000 but lowered to 50,000 midyear; the FY 2021 refugee ceiling was originally 15,000 but increased to 62,500 midyear.

Sources: US Departments of State, Homeland Security, and Health and Human Services, "Proposed Refugee Admissions for Fiscal Year," various years; Migration Policy Institute analysis of the State Department's Worldwide Refugee Admissions Processing System data, available online.

APPENDIX III

CHEEER

Too often I get asked for a playbook for how we do what we do. Sometimes I get stumped trying to answer complicated questions because what we do is not profound; it's actually really simple. At Fugees Academy, we use the acronym CHEEER to remind us of our core values.

CHILDHOOD

Schools are about children. Being a child is about having fun. Too often we forget to have fun. We focus on discipline and sitting in a class for eight hours. It's important to schedule time for play.

For Halloween, our students vote on a theme and create costumes over the course of a month. We've been stormtroopers and Yodas, Mad Hatters and rabbits, hamburgers and French fries. Students learn how to sew and use a hot glue gun. They paint one another's faces. We order pizza the night of trick-or-treating and the whole school goes together.

Wahid's first Halloween was at age thirteen. The other kids told him everything he needed to know — knock on the door, take the candy, say thank you. If porch lights are off, keep walking. After a few hours, the students came back ready to head home and take stock of their sugary haul.

"What time tomorrow, Coach?" asked Wahid.

"We don't have a game tomorrow," I replied, a little confused.

"No, what time are we trick-or-treating?"

"Oh, trick-or-treating is only today, just one day of the year."

Wahid's face fell. "Why don't we do this every day?" he asked.

I think of Wahid a lot because he was on to something. Fun should be a daily habit.

HUMILITY

Every semester, when we get our academic progress test scores back, teachers, coaches, and administrators sit down as a team and take a hard look at them. We also have an outside data analyst give us an objective read. Then we have an honest and hard conversation about everything. Which students did we not reach? What are we going to change about how we teach to improve on our results?

Our students average a 2.3 grade level jump every year, far exceeding their peers, but that's often not good enough to get them to grade level. Our work is difficult, and it is humbling. You can be a master teacher, but our students will force you to get even better. That's why our teachers have to learn from one another across subjects and grade levels. What methods do our art teachers use that our English teachers could implement? And vice versa? We encourage our teachers to have a beginner's mindset, to always look for ways they can improve their craft.

We are kind and respectful, but at the same time, we don't have to worry about hurting one another's feelings. Everyone understands that we cannot let ego and hurt feelings get in the way of the common goal.

We cannot be stubborn and continue pressing the gas pedal if the car is careening off the cliff. If our data shows that our students aren't improving, it's on us to figure out why and change how we do things to make sure they are. We harm our students if we put blinders on to any mediocrity around us. Our team is only as strong as it is humble.

EQUITY

Every student in our school plays soccer, every student learns to play an instrument, every student does art. We eliminate all the barriers to access: cost, time, and transportation. One of the simplest ways we do this is by incorporating these activities into the school day. Practice is held immediately after school, and we provide annual equipment for each student. Similarly, we never put a student or parent in a position to say that they can't participate because of cost or schedule.

Everyone at school eats together and we all eat the same meal. We sit together and talk and take a real break. No one is allowed to bring their own meal. Our students are happy with this system. Ask them why we do it and they will tell you that it's because we're all equal. No one brings in food others can't afford. No one is better than or less than. This puts the responsibility on us — right where it should be — to provide healthy meals that cater to all the dietary restrictions of our students and staff. The vast majority of schools may not be able to follow our exact example here, but every school can examine the ways meals reinforce inequity, and the way they might be used to grow community.

EXCELLENCE

Our schools have a reputation in the community. Kids who don't go to our school say things like "If you mess up, they are on you," or "If you miss school, they call your house and come get you," or "They know how to speak one hundred languages and can talk to your parents." Obviously, I am very proud of this reputation. I think every school should have the same one.

We expect our students to be the best they can be. Always improving. We set the bar high, and once they hit it, we raise it even higher. We expect our students to say good morning and thank you and have their shirts tucked in. We don't accept late work, and students are not let into class if they are more than five minutes late. The rules are clear and everyone is held to the same standard. Every teacher enforces the same code of conduct; we are all part of the same team.

We don't, however, expect a newly arrived illiterate eleven-year-old to perform at grade level. We meet them where they are at and take time to teach the fundamentals. That student will never get an A in sixth grade because an A is for excellent grade-level work. That student will also never get an F if they show up and try.

If a student gets in a fight, they take responsibility for those they harmed. The person they hit, the class they interrupted, the teacher they disrespected. Our students stand in front of their community and ask permission to come back into the classroom. Everyone gets to ask questions about what happened and why and how it will be avoided in the future. Our high expectations for our students mean they have high expectations for one another.

EMPOWERMENT

We often get asked by area middle or high school students or their parents if they can tutor or coach our kids. My answer is always no. Having other same-age students tutor ours would create a giving-receiving dynamic that reinforces the same old power structures that tell our students they are less than.

We rely on a mix of college and community volunteers for tutoring, but we take every chance we can get to let our own older students and coaches serve as tutors so they can see themselves as leaders and role models. We develop our leaders from within; our priority, our North Star, is the kids in our building. Our school is for refugees by refugees.

The ultimate goal of empowering our students is that once they leave us they don't need us anymore. We don't create a cycle of dependence with programs that support them after they leave our schools.

RESPECT

During our teacher orientation, we spend hours learning how to pronounce our students' names. We don't Americanize the names or shorten them for our own comfort or because it's easier; we simply take a few extra hours practicing how to say them. We rely on our parents and teachers who are native speakers of those languages to help us learn. Our last day of orientation culminates in a meal hosted by the parents in their homes, which allows our teachers to see and experience the richness of their students' culture, family, and food. We cannot get respect if we have not earned it.

Our staff is continuously learning about different cultures and customs through time with family, holidays, and student assignments. It's so vital that they understand all the different identities our students are straddling and show that they respect and honor each one.

For an expanded version of CHEEER, go to www.fugeesfamily .org.

NOTES

CHAPTER 8

Paul Tough's *Whatever It Takes: Geoffrey Canada's Quest to Change Harlem and America,* Houghton Mifflin Harcourt, 2014, and Jonathan Kozol's classic *Savage Inequalities: Children in America's Schools,* Crown, 2012, are two books that have been formative for my work.

The Stanford Graduate School of Education's paper mentioned is Kenji Hakuta, Yuko Goto Butler, and Daria Witt's "How Long Does It Take English Learners to Attain Proficiency?" The University of California Linguistic Minority Research Institute, Policy Report, 2000–1, https://web.stanford.edu/~hakuta/Publications/(2000)%20-%20HOW%20LONG%20DOES%20IT%20TAKE%20ENGLISH%20LEARNERS%20TO%20ATTAIN%20PR.pdf.

CHAPTER 9

The *New York Times* article mentioned is Keith Meatto's "Still Separate, Still Unequal: Teaching about School Segregation and Educational Inequity," *New York Times,* May 2, 2019, https://www.nytimes.com/2019/05/02/learning/lesson-plans/still-separate-still-unequal-teaching-about-school-segregation-and-educational-inequality.html.

CHAPTER 11

The source for the information on teacher training in Finland is Sari Muhonen's "In Finland it's easier to become a doctor or lawyer than a teacher — Here's why," *The Hechinger Report,* October 16, 2017, https://hechingerreport.org/teacher-voice-in-finland-its-easier-to-become-a-doctor-or-lawyer-than-a-teacher-heres-why/.

The source regarding teacher training in Singapore is "Singapore: Teacher and Principal Quality," National Center on Education and the Economy's Center on International Education Benchmarking, https://ncee.org/what-we-do/center-on-international-education-benchmarking/top-performing-countries/singapore-overview-2/singapore-teacher-and-principal-quality/.

CHAPTER 12

The research on the importance of adults in children's lives mentioned in this chapter is from David Murphey, Tawana Bandy, Hannah Schmitz, and Kristin A. Moore's "Caring Adults: Important for Positive Child Well-Being," Childtrends.org, 2013, https://www.childtrends.org/wp-content/uploads/2013/12/2013-54CaringAdults.pdf.

CHAPTER 13

The two books by important researcher/writers on childhood adversity and trauma mentioned in this chapter are Dr. Bessel van der Kolk's *The Body Keeps the Score: Brain, Mind, and Body in the Healing of Trauma,* Penguin Books, 2015, and Nadine Burke Harris's *The Deepest Well: Healing the Long-Term Effects of Childhood Adversity,* Houghton Mifflin Harcourt, 2019.

The statistics about pediatric drug prescriptions mentioned in this chapter are from Frieda Wiley's "Psychotropic Drugs in Pediatrics: Looking at the Whole Child," *Drug Topics Journal* 162, no. 12, December 21, 2018, https://www.drugtopics.com/view/psychotropic-drugs-pediatrics-looking-whole-child.

CHAPTER 14

Zaretta L. Hammond's work has been a touchstone; her book is *Culturally Responsive Teaching and the Brain: Promoting Authentic Engagement and Rigor Among Culturally and Linguistically Diverse Students,* Corwin, 2014.

CHAPTER 15

The article on grade inflation mentioned in this chapter is Tom Lindsay's "The 'Other' College Scandal: Grade Inflation Has Turned Transcripts into Monopoly Money," *Forbes,* March 30, 2019, https://www.forbes.com/sites/tomlindsay/2019/03/30/the-other-college-scandal-grade-inflation-has-turned-transcripts-into-monopoly-money/?sh=2bf839404182.

APPENDIX III

For an expanded version of CHEEER, please visit www.fugeesfamily.org.

ABOUT

MARINER BOOKS

MARINER BOOKS traces its beginnings to 1832 when William Ticknor cofounded the Old Corner Bookstore in Boston, from which he would run the legendary firm Ticknor and Fields, publisher of Ralph Waldo Emerson, Harriet Beecher Stowe, Nathaniel Hawthorne, and Henry David Thoreau. Following Ticknor's death, Henry Oscar Houghton acquired Ticknor and Fields and, in 1880, formed Houghton Mifflin, which later merged with venerable Harcourt Publishing to form Houghton Mifflin Harcourt. HarperCollins purchased HMH's trade publishing business in 2021 and reestablished their storied lists and editorial team under the name Mariner Books.

Uniting the legacies of Houghton Mifflin, Harcourt Brace, and Ticknor and Fields, Mariner Books continues one of the great traditions in American bookselling. Our imprints have introduced an incomparable roster of enduring classics, including Hawthorne's *The Scarlet Letter*, Thoreau's *Walden*, Willa Cather's *O Pioneers!*, Virginia Woolf's *To the Lighthouse*, W.E.B. Du Bois's *Black Reconstruction*, J.R.R. Tolkien's *The Lord of the Rings*, Carson McCullers's *The Heart Is a Lonely Hunter*, Ann Petry's *The Narrows*, George Orwell's *Animal Farm* and *Nineteen Eighty-Four*, Rachel Carson's *Silent Spring*, Margaret Walker's *Jubilee*, Italo Calvino's *Invisible Cities*, Alice Walker's *The Color Purple*, Margaret Atwood's *The Handmaid's Tale*, Tim O'Brien's *The Things They Carried*, Philip Roth's *The Plot Against America*, Jhumpa Lahiri's *Interpreter of Maladies*, and many others. Today Mariner Books remains proudly committed to the craft of fine publishing established nearly two centuries ago at the Old Corner Bookstore.